TWITCH

CREATING, GROWING, & MONETIZING YOUR LIVESTREAM

Table of Contents

018 Act I: Broadcasters and Their Tools

Foreword

If you're reading this book, you already know what Twitch is. Dan and Kim will take you through how it works and how to succeed as a broadcaster. We'd like to talk about why Twitch is important—both as a new form of entertainment and a new driver of celebrity, and also because it is reshaping how games are made.

We are witnessing the birth of a new kind of celebrity, and it's a fascinating time to be thinking about livestreaming. On a basic level, Twitch recreates the feeling gamers used to have when, as kids, we gathered around a Super Nintendo, four or five at a time, taking turns playing a game together. Our victories were shared victories. Our challenges were put to the group to be solved. What we discovered, without realizing it, was simple:

Games are better together.

Our old friends are now adults scattered across the country, but in Twitch we can find new friends to share the same experiences. We form bonds with our favorite broadcasters as well as our fellow viewers. We meet the stars and their communities at conventions and fan meetups. Twitch makes games better together again.

What seems to strike people most about watching Twitch streams is the interactivity. Never before has there been a broadcast show that can actually talk *back* to you. Not only are you watching someone play games, but you are talking with them, asking questions, providing advice, and generally being a part of the show. Imagine watching Oprah or Ellen, and at the start of the program, they say hello, by name, to each and every person that comes in and sits down.

In Hollywood, the person you see on the screen is a facade, a carefully crafted persona designed to project a certain image. An actor or musician plays an outward-facing role easily, because their interactions with the public are so limited. For Twitch broadcasters, who interact with the public for six or more hours a day, every day, it's almost impossible to hide your true personality. If you are quick to anger, it comes out. If you are prone to using foul language, it comes out. It you say racist or immature things, it comes out. The person you see on the screen may be putting on a show... but they are doing so as the person they actually are. They connect with their audiences in meaningful ways. They make friends. They occasionally even fall in love. It's amazing to see people so willing to authentically share their lives with others.

For broadcasters, there are the added dimensions of fame and fortune. Gamers are a competitive group of people. Since the early days of arcades, we've tried to prove that we're the best, through high scores, speed records, or being the first to take down a particularly difficult boss. Twitch allows broadcasters to demonstrate their skills live, with a perfect video record of their accomplishments. No longer is the only proof of your world-first boss takedown a screenshot. Now, the entire process is recorded for all time.

As broadcasters have garnered audiences in the tens and, now, hundreds of thousands, brands have taken note—they offer promotions and sponsorships that can easily reach six figures. Much like professional athletes, some broadcasters now make more money from these sponsorships than they do from their organic channel income (ads, subscriptions, and tips). We're seeing the first generation of Twitch-made millionaires now and witnessing them reap the rewards and pay the prices that come along with this level of notoriety.

All of these changes are fascinating, but nothing about Twitch streaming is as world-changing as the effect it is having on the game industry. In Twitch, developers have found an amazing and effective tool for awareness—but also one that is harder to control than any previous form of marketing. Twitch broadcasters, almost universally, began their careers as fans. And, unencumbered by the years and years of harsh realities of working at game companies, they feel perfectly free to speak their minds, to challenge the status quo, and to demand that games be more like what they and their audiences want to play.

In recent years, we've seen content creators across Twitch and YouTube completely reshape which games can succeed. It may surprise you to learn, but *Fortnite* can attribute almost all of its success to Twitch broadcasters, who found it a fun alternative to *PlayerUnknown's Battlegrounds*, which itself had been seen as an improvement over *H1Z1*. Each of those games made millions due to the nonstop promotion by Twitch's top stars—and each felt the pain of being abandoned in favor of the next "hype game."

The same can be said for indie darlings such as *FTL: Faster Than Light*, *They Are Billions*, *RimWorld*, *Stardew Valley*, *Terraria*, *Goat Simulator*, and so many more. These are games that major publishers would never have considered making ten years ago... but now are discussed in the boardrooms of EA, Activision, and Tencent.

Oh, and if you've heard of a little thing called esports? Guess where the majority of that plays out: Twitch.

These are still the early days. We are witnessing completely new types of content, such as when an IRL streamer walks down the street interviewing people, or someone like Kitboga calls Indian tech support scammers to waste their time. Body painting, cosplay, game creation, art, roleplaying, and a hundred other ideas are playing out live on Twitch.tv, offering up their ideas to the masses to see which of them are well-received.

This democratization of content is fascinating. It leads to better games, better celebrities and, ultimately, better entertainment.

We're glad you'll be coming along for the ride.

– Jenn and Omeed Dariani

Introduction

Welcome

On the most serious note possible, welcome to the Twitch book. "The Twitch book" has been a staple of our vocabulary for a few months now, as we crammed on, writing and creating this project. As the wonderful people at Prima Games, Kim (Sabre) and I (Danotage) worked very hard to bring you the most comprehensive information possible to help you maximize your Twitch channel's reach and power. There are a few things to know before you dive in.

Firstly, as most everyone is well aware, the gaming industry moves at lightning speed, so we endeavored to bring you the latest information before things changed in the middle of writing. Nevertheless, a small overhaul of some options occurred within the few months during which we wrote this book. Our primary goal was to focus on timeless advice that would help your career for the long haul. We provide philosophies and strategies, rather than focus on merely what's hot at the current moment in time.

Secondly, we intend this book to be a how-to without being a how-to. That is to say, we don't provide a cookie-cutter formula to become successful on Twitch—that is literally impossible to do. Instead, we explain the mindset you need to develop your personality, channel, brand, opportunities, and everything else your creative mind might envision. Kim and I are not the biggest broadcasters on Twitch. However, we've developed opportunities that sustain us on Twitch while working with broadcasters and video games, and cultivating wisdom from the broadcasting world.

Finally, this book is meant to be fun. I mean, in the end, Twitch is about video games, art, and community—no part of that should ever be boring, stale, or too serious. Some chapters may be less exciting than others, but they may keep you from losing your livelihood while pursuing this as a viable career option. Whatever happens with your Twitch career, if you have fun, enjoy what you do, and can still afford to eat real food, then you should never stop doing what you love. Keep your head up and keep sharpening your skills. The results will come and your hard work will always pay off.

Okay, now get to reading. A lot of information is ready for you to soak up.

Meet the Authors

Dan "Danotage" Herrera

Dan has lived his life in many chapters. He spent part of his life right out of high school as a pro gamer, then as a radio DJ. He opened another chapter as a full-time author, and now is a full-time broadcaster on Twitch as well as an author of numerous strategy guides for Prima Games. Although he always enjoyed creating entertainment and content within the video game realm, it wasn't until he came upon the opportunity to raise money for charity that he turned his attention to Twitch. The chance to see how much money a new broadcaster with a small following could raise in a single day inspired his start on Twitch. With that objective in mind, he began to build a community of a few hundred followers before the charity efforts commenced. From 2015 on, Dan never stopped streaming and has loved every moment of it. Having raised over $75,000 for charities supporting children, military veterans around the globe, and animals in need, Dan now makes a living as a broadcaster while growing and making new friends every day.

twitch.tv/danotage

youtube.com/danotage

twitter.com/danotage

instagram.com/danotage

facebook.com/danotage

Kimberly "Sabre" Weigend

Kimberly Weigend works as a producer in a AAA video game studio, and believes that livestreaming and interactive entertainment will play an important role in the future of gaming. She is a former member of a Twitch Partnered livestream team devoted to competitive and casual gaming, through which she raised thousands of dollars for charities and mentored other women trying to break into the games industry. She has created many gaming related YouTube videos with millions of views, co-hosted live E3 pre-shows, given GDC talks, and continues to stream on her personal channel on Twitch. With her professional background in business and management, Kimberly dedicates her time to building great gaming experiences and keeps a pulse on gaming trends, new technology, and interactive media.

twitch.tv/Sabre_AP   twitter/Sabre_AP
instagram/Sabre_AP

What Is Twitch?

No matter the level of broadcaster you are, folks will ask you this question until Twitch becomes a mainstream media source to traditional viewers. Inquisitive people ask this question for many different reasons. We'll delve into these reasons in this chapter and throughout the rest of this book. The question itself, "What is Twitch?" may be one reason you're reading this publication. Or, perhaps you're one of the millions of people who watch Twitch and you seek advice on how to become a streamer. Anyone with an internet connection, located in any part of the world, can watch any of the millions of broadcasters who create live content daily with minimal delay. On the same note, anyone with a reliable internet connection can stream their content to the Twitch platform.

Why Twitch?

Although one can select several other platforms to stream and create content, only a small number are viable for monetization. When we decided to write this book, we elected to focus on the Twitch platform because, even though there are many shared ideas and strategies, Twitch is the leader in the streaming scene.

As you know, this industry changes regularly as new technological advances affect how streamers conduct their business. As such, Twitch continually seeks to better serve the talent who utilize their platform. Twitch strives to provide streamers more opportunities to grow and monetize their brands. As both observers and talent on Twitch, we have come to know and love the platform, but we've also experienced the growing pains that you may currently be experiencing. This book shares our knowledge and provides many strategies you can use to improve your streaming experience.

History and Evolution

Justin.tv

Like most major tech businesses, Justin.tv started with a good idea, a good investment, and a lot of passion and hard work. Justin Kan, the founder of Justin.tv, wrote in a *Tech Crunch* article that "Starting Justin.tv was a bad idea, but I'm glad we did it anyway." Emmett Shear, the CEO of Twitch, was working with Kan on a calendar application known as Kiko when things started to look grim for them both. They weren't making enough money to pay themselves, so they considered making major changes to their lives and possibly switching industries.

As they discussed new ideas about Kiko, Kan asked his partner what it might be like if people could listen to the conversation they were currently having. They wondered whether their project strategy discussion would be interesting to others who might have had similar conversations, or to those who wanted to hear something new. This very quickly evolved into the idea of watching people who filmed themselves live. Several proven events had already demonstrated that folks were fascinated with other people's lives. Reality television was in full swing, and despite suspicions about whether programs truly represented reality, fans still tuned in.

In short order, Justin and Emmett received $50,000 in funding from their friends, Paul and Robert Morris. They told Justin, "[We'll] fund it just to see you make a fool of yourself." Now they had to develop a video platform that users would be interested in and want to watch for extended periods. Six months later, they recruited two of their other co-founders, Kyle Vogt and Michael Seibel. More or less flying by the seat of their pants with little money and no plan, the Justin.tv team created a platform that allowed a large number of people to watch others live their lives.

Twitch Transition

Although Justin.tv is where this all started, Twitch has evolved many times since its creation. However, the beginning may be the biggest evolution to date, next to the introduction of partnerships and IRL (In Real Life).

In June 2011, Justin.tv's creators were producing more than 300 live videos, about 4.5 hours of recorded video, and about 3.2 million unique visitors to the website every month (*TechCrunch*, Rao, 2011). At this time in online video streaming, it represented decent growth and significant numbers for a startup. CEO Michael Seibel believed the platform didn't have a specific purpose and that the company could pursue many avenues to increase its growth. One vital growth strategy was the partnership with major esports.

Esports viewership was on the rise, capturing the attention of tech media and entire gaming communities. Riding the esports wave was perhaps one of the wisest moves a streaming platform could make. Partnering with games such as *Halo: Reach*, *StarCraft II*, *World of Warcraft*, and *Call of Duty: Black Ops*, Twitch could provide gameplay commentary to viewers already on their platform as well as the communities that cared about these games. The launch of Twitch also launched the streaming of E3 (Electronic Entertainment Expo) content outside of review sites. GameSpot was among the first companies to partner with Twitch; they were brought on to provide 90 hours of content from E3.

Twitch's new objective was to bring a gaming-focused platform to viewers seeking entertainment. Gaming entertainment now comes in all shapes and sizes, and it has been Twitch's mainstay for some time. Twitch has introduced different content categories since its early days, but even now gaming is the ultimate focus.

Early Partners

Even on Justin.tv, many talented broadcasters and personalities flocked to the platform. So much so, that the company needed to help their content creators promote their platform even more. Without additional support from the platform, content creators may have continued producing subject matter for their fans a while longer, but in the long run they would need a deeper relationship with Twitch.

This prompted creation of the original partnership program. The first rendition of the program bore no resemblance to today's iteration. There was no method to monetarily subscribe to a channel, and "cheering" via Twitch Bits did not yet exist. The options to monetize one's channel and develop a career from within the platform were limited. At this early stage, sponsorships for talent were possible, but many content creators didn't realize streaming on Twitch could become a career. Many broadcasters practiced their esports games and showed off classic titles to gain an audience. Soon thereafter, broadcasters began speedrunning communities, charity fundraisers, and full-on playthroughs of the latest games to hit the market. As the variety of content and its creators broadened, so did Twitch's desire to develop their partnership program.

The Boom

In an intense growth period, Twitch began to attract talent from all over the world, having already lured a variety of entertaining broadcasters, like MANVSGAME and Kreyg, among others. It was obvious that Twitch had the talent to be keep its audience satisfied. However, every business needs a way to maintain growth and build with a scale in mind. Twitch wasn't necessarily in the market for bigger partnerships to help with scale. Instead, the target was a larger mass of entertaining broadcasters eager to create content on a regular basis. This large wave of new partners quickly developed a solid base for Twitch, giving viewers a wider variety of talent to watch.

This influx of content creators triggered a boom in broadcaster and viewer traffic on the platform. In turn, this produced a strange culture in which broadcasters thought more about becoming Twitch partners than creating the best possible content for their communities. Unfortunately, at least one of this book's authors became similarly distracted. The positive side effect was that, after some time, many realized this approach didn't produce lasting success. As new broadcasters arrived on the scene, many of them did their research and learned what it took to develop a community. This was still a big growth period for Twitch and its entire staff, so they were learning along with the content creators and viewers. Twitch observed that talent was thinking this way and began to expand its partnerships team, which prompted a deeper analysis into who might work well with the team; they began paying attention to specific streamers.

As the end of the boom drew near, Twitch started to emerge as a main media source for many viewers. Nevertheless, Twitch livestreams represented only a small portion of the content viewed on the internet. Although many replaced their normal television viewing by watching streams, the audience was small compared to the vast size of the video gaming community. Gaming was (and is) extremely popular and one of the world's biggest industries, but its audience largely played video games rather than watching them via a broadcaster. This was about to change from the broadcasting side; it was simply a matter of time. Now, with a solid base of broadcasters, a niche but growing audience, and well-known sponsors, Twitch had the basic foundation to create a brand new media.

Amazon Purchase

Near the end of 2014, Amazon announced it would purchase Twitch, making it an Amazon subsidiary. For the first few years, Twitch was barely affected by the purchase. In fact, it was allowed to hire staff, expand its teams, and sign more partners with ease. Shortly after the purchase came the introduction of Creative as an official Twitch category, which became a huge hit. Streamers had been broadcasting creative content on their channels for a short time, but it fell under relatively tight restrictions. All creative activity had to be gaming related, and it was extremely difficult to be discovered as a broadcaster taking this approach. On October 28, 2015, Twitch released a blog post detailing a new landing page for the Creative category. Twitch introduced the category with Adobe as its promotional partner, launching the program with full force to the community that enjoyed this type of live entertainment. To help Creative broadcasters become known, Twitch introduced tags to stream titles, which allowed viewers to find very specific types of Creative streams. These innovations brought on another boom, this time consisting of Creative partners. The launch of Creative was Twitch's first step into expanding beyond the world of gaming.

The Creative category was only the beginning of Twitch becoming one of the world's biggest tech media empires, following suit with its new parent company, Amazon. In March 2017, a few years after it introduced Creative, Twitch launched an IRL category, or "In Real Life." Similar to the way Justin.tv began, Twitch added this category to allow people to stream whenever and wherever. Twitch wanted to give broadcasters a chance to appease audiences that followed them for their own brand and not necessarily for the games they played. These fans wanted to watch their favorite content creator and, given the choice, everything the broadcaster did on a daily basis. Indeed, IRL-type content is the main reason Justin.tv started in the first place, so today the IRL category is a version of Justin.tv, only larger, with many more options. With a great deal more restrictions on content (which is a necessity), Twitch allows broadcasters to stream anything they want—within reason. This gives people all over the world an opportunity to entertain an audience by doing something they love.

Ninja

"Ninja is the Rock of Twitch," stated talented veteran broadcaster Ben "ProfessorBroman" Bowman in his description of Tyler "Ninja" Blevins—his statement was an accurate one. Ben was saying that Ninja was the first crossover star from Twitch to another major platform or audience. Like Dwayne "The Rock" Johnson going from wrestling to film, Ninja is recognized by the music industry and esports, and he makes appearances on the national news, in effect representing all Twitch broadcasters.

The reason we discuss Ninja in this chapter is, whether or not he's the true reason for a major evolution in Twitch, he has become the face of said evolution. Through thousands of entertainers' hard work on the Twitch platform, people can now experience gaming as entertainment by watching it live instead of playing the games themselves. With the increasing influence broadcasters have on the gaming market, more and more publishers see value in advertising with talent such as Ninja. Tyler has worked with many major companies, challenging the perception that Twitch is a niche market. It now reaches the eyes and ears of traditional consumers. Although promotions and professionally sponsored content have existed on streaming platforms for some time, it always took a lot of work to convince companies of its power, even if they were familiar with Twitch. Once Ninja broke the mold with his famous *Fortnite* stream along with hip-hop artist Drake, companies that knew about Twitch became much more interested, and those that didn't at least indulged in the conversation.

It's important to note that Ninja didn't come out of nowhere. He streamed on Twitch for several years before his fame exploded. He also played *Halo* professionally for some time, which helped him hone the skills he needed to play *Fortnite*. As one of the factors that helped Ninja's celebrity rise to an unprecedented level, *Fortnite* provided a perfect mix, balancing all-ages gaming with the battle royale genre. It had the backing of a AAA company able to push the game's marketing to a large scale. With Ninja as the top entertainer in the *Fortnite* category, the company worked very closely with him, rocketing both parties' marketing to new heights.

Act I: Broadcasters and Their Tools

Introduction

Long ago, broadcasters played video games for an internet audience from their bedrooms, with roommates making noise in the other room, often using nothing more than a headset microphone and a laptop camera more suited to Skyping your grandmother. Does any of this sound familiar? Probably not, because today you're starting off on much better footing than those early broadcasters. For an extraordinary number of Twitch streamers, this is how their careers began. My co-author Kim and I started streaming on Twitch for competitive gaming, charity, and the personal need to cultivate a positive and goal-focused community while providing at least a little entertainment. When a lot of us started, there weren't many products to help broadcasters stream at a higher quality, or at least few that were affordable for anyone starting from scratch.

The early days of Justin.tv and Twitch were very much like the Wild West. Broadcasters took what they had and fired content at the wall to see what stuck. Using inferior microphones and cameras that, if you squinted hard enough, you could decipher the pixels and identify what you were looking at. Although we may be exaggerating a bit, for some the only choice was whatever they could get their hands on. This remains true for some even today.

This chapter explores broadcasters and the tools they use in addition to common practices to improve your stream. Keep in mind that this chapter doesn't cover all the tools by any means, and there's no reason you have to use them all. In fact, you don't need to use any of these tools; instead, relying on your own methods can provide just as much opportunity to succeed as others on this platform.

This chapter will help you start streaming to Twitch and possibly take you beyond your current technical limitations. Regardless of your stream's technological and audiovisual quality, you must provide an engaging broadcast that people find entertaining—the tools can help you only so much. The reverse also applies; you can have a wonderful personality but fail to upgrade your tech to keep pace with your channel's growth. The upside with the latter is that you don't need much to keep your audiovisual quality very high, especially if you don't use a camera or special effects.

The Basics

Streaming Software

There is no stream without software. It's safe to say that every Twitch stream is being pushed through some kind of streaming-specific software. Whether it's one of the common apps that most broadcasters use or more specialized software, they all combine multiple sources into one video signal to be streamed. That video is transmitted to a Twitch server, called an ingest server, after which Twitch sends the same video to all of the servers for everyone to watch. This precludes the need for a direct connection from the streamer to the viewer. It's all about the viewer's connection to the nearest Twitch server, which helps you as the broadcaster reach the largest possible audience, at least in theory. The platform is designed to reach the maximum number of people around the world, but the streamer's setup determine's his or her reach. We cover these details later in a section devoted to settings.

Hardware

Thankfully, it doesn't take a monster gaming PC to get a stream online, but you can't do it using what industry pros call a "potato." The term refers to a computer that essentially serves as a paper weight. Often, a potato can run simple programs, but not very many simultaneously. This is noteworthy because that's what needs to happen for a stream to be live on Twitch. The streaming software does the heavy lifting (i.e., running the processes needed to make the broadcast look right), but your system's processor, or CPU, makes sure it all runs smoothly.

In order to produce a high-quality broadcast, you don't need a dozen fancy graphics onscreen at the same time. It looks really cool when DrDisrespect walks into his locker room to chat with his audience while the news ticker runs in the background, the backdrop on his ultra key is flawless, and the helicopter on the roof has the engine running, ready to take off. It also looks amazing when CohhCarnage gets a subscriber and his logo performs a sweet animation, showing the subscriber's name. All of these things are possible, but realize that something has to process those animations and background data. Some technologies can help relieve your local CPU by processing elements off-site and just pushing the video to a browser source on your streaming software. But even then your PC still has to run it. Remember that we're just talking about the stream—you still need to run the game.

Of course, we want to educate you, not scare you away from streaming. We also want to spare you from pouring a fortune into equipment before you know whether you really need it. There are many schools of thought regarding where to start in terms of equipment. One popular setup employs two PCs, one for gaming and one for processing the stream. This probably isn't the best idea for newcomers, especially those with a limited budget, but it's an option. One benefit of having two PCs is that if something goes wrong with one, it's great to have a backup, even if it's not the ideal setup. Most two-PC setups consist of a nice gaming PC and a middle-of-the-road machine just powerful enough to run the processes needed for your stream. Although this scenario makes the backup option a little less viable, it's still feasible for a resource-light game stream.

Camera and Lighting

The Camera

Having a camera is not a requirement, nor is it even important to some streamers. As we've stated before, using a camera is not the reason you will become—or not become—a successful broadcaster. For those who want to use a camera, there are plenty of options. USB webcams have been the norm since the beginning of Twitch and will probably continue to be standard for most broadcasts. USB cameras, like the ones from Logitech and Creative, are extremely good and quite affordable. Companies like Razer and Turtle Beach, commonly known as producers of external accessories, also offer products specifically for broadcasters. The great thing about these affordable options is that they're essentially plug and play.

The Choice

One reason to use a camera is that it makes it easier to sell who you are to your audience. As you may already know, when you start your career as a broadcaster it can be difficult to create engaging content, especially if you haven't done it before. Using a camera facilitates making a connection with your audience. This connection is part of what we mean when we refer to engaging content on Twitch. Because Twitch is a live platform, your audience is always a revolving door of viewers coming in and out of your stream. This means you have a short period of time to capture each new viewer who gives your channel a shot. This is the strength of having a camera, but if you are an engaging speaker, you can convey your personality without using a camera and achieve a similar effect.

Ultra Key

If you use a camera, another decision will affect the look of your onscreen setup. Of course, it's important to place the camera in the right spot, but that's entirely broadcaster preference. Remember that it's best to make the stream look the way you want it and stick with it. So, the next question is whether or not to use an ultra key, or a green screen, to replace your studio's background, minimizing the onscreen footprint of your in-studio camera feed. There is no right or wrong way to go here; it's entirely up to you as a broadcaster. However, many streamers feel using a green screen significantly changes the dynamic of a stream, for better or worse.

Using an ultra key has a considerable effect on how viewers connect with the broadcaster. Streamers typically approach using ultra key in one of two ways. One approach is to force the viewer to focus exclusively on the broadcaster and what is happening in-game. A second approach is to give the viewer an open window into the space where the broadcaster works. Stylistically, an ultra key makes it much easier to keep one's stream visually clean and consistent because the only elements that really change are the broadcaster and what he or she wears. Without an ultra key, additional variables play a part when you use a camera: What's happening in the studio's background? Is it an interesting background? Does the environment give the viewer an idea about the broadcaster before he or she even speaks? Consider these factors when you decide whether to use an ultra key.

Finally, many broadcasters give a lot of thought to lighting. It's very important to ensure viewers can see you properly. Furthermore, you can use lighting to set a specific mood for your type of stream. You can do a lot with lighting if you aren't using an ultra key. Conversely, if you do use one, your lighting must be near perfect, or it will be obvious that something is amiss. It's almost essential to light the ultra key screen behind the broadcaster separately, otherwise shadows can create noise and make the screen's presence obvious. Of course, viewers will still know when you're using an ultra key. The goal is to make the viewer forget that a camera is filming the broadcaster. If the screen and broadcaster are illuminated separately, the lighting will be even and balanced for the entire frame.

Your Channel, Your Settings

Taking Ownership

First and foremost, you are the master of your domain. Whatever the circumstance, there's a good chance tools exist to help you control what happens—and what's allowed to happen—in your channel. When you're busy streaming and making sure the content you produce is the best it can be, it's easy to let things like simple settings, filters, and banned words slip through the cracks. It's smart to spend some time exploring the Twitch website's settings and menu tools—adjust them to your liking. Some aspects of security and filtering may not be immediately obvious. This chapter provides insight into topics to consider, such as what you might want to filter out, or how to focus your channel's chat so it's productive and friendly to a specific community or age group.

Profile

Let's start with the easy part: your profile. Your Twitch profile is important for several reasons. For starters, your profile picture is the first thing people see when they browse for channels to watch. The channel description gives viewers their first glimpse into who you are and what your channel is all about. Your profile is important because it's probably the quickest way for others to determine what kind of channel you have. With your profile picture and bio, you can establish and control your outward-facing persona. Viewing your clips is another way viewers can get a glimpse into your channel, but you don't control how clips from your channel are taken. Just remember that even well-meaning content can be taken out of context and painted with a distorted brush. Your profile is where you can paint a picture with your own custom brush.

Profile Picture

Obviously, a profile picture provides the quickest way to visually identify a streamer, whether you're visiting another broadcaster's channel or posting your channel on other platforms. It's a good idea to use the same image everywhere to be consistent with your brand, but it's okay to deviate for specific reasons if the need arises.

So, how do you select your Twitch profile picture? A few strategies have proven effective, but it's important that you are the subject of the picture, especially if you use a camera when you broadcast. This comes in handy if someone you've recently met, either at a convention or some other venue, happens upon your profile picture browsing Twitch for a stream to watch. Also, using a "real" image of yourself makes it much easier for everyone to make an instant visual connection, even if they've never seen you before. We recommend using a close-up photo with good lighting, as the image size on the site is rather small. If you have a high-quality frame or screen from your stream setup, crop the screenshot to show you and nothing else to depict you in your "natural habitat."

Many people who don't use a camera when they broadcast use a logo as their profile picture. A good logo can represent your broadcast and your brand, particularly one that doesn't contain words, your name, or excessive detail. The profile picture is so small that you can't fit much on the canvas that viewers will be able to read. Geometric, high-contrast, and clearly defined logos work best as profile pictures. Whether you use a logo or a photo of yourself, the easier you make identifying what's in the image, the more likely people who view your profile will recognize you.

Profile Banner

Compared to your profile picture, your profile banner is much larger. This is where you can provide more information about your channel, instead of trying to force it all into your profile picture. Nevertheless, apply similar standards to your profile banner; use a clear image that's easy for a visually oriented audience to read and recognize. The profile banner is a great place to display your social media accounts and other information that remains static for extended periods. Avoid changing your profile picture and banner too often, unless you decide to make a big visual change to your brand. It's perfectly fine for these images to go unchanged for long durations, as persistent branding can make you easier to recognize among viewers.

Profile Settings

Username/Display Name

Arguably the most prominent part of your brand is your name. Your name is how everyone identifies you. We emphasize this because your brand is how you will be recognized in the entertainment industry. Your brand is more than your name, of course, but your name is where everything starts. If you haven't already established a name/username on any other media platform, take some time to brainstorm for one. Your username doesn't have to mean anything, nor does it even need to make sense. You may want to make it easy to read (possibly without numbers mixed in) and one you can build a visual brand around. Naturally, make sure you don't mind introducing yourself with the name you choose.

Note that you can change your username as long as you meet Twitch's criteria. Changing your name won't necessarily change your brand, but know that it may cause some confusion if you don't formally get the word out. One reason to change your name is to better align it with a brand you create. For example, in 2017 ashley66444 changed her name to Smashley to remove the numbers, which some people probably considered arbitrary. This change actually strengthened her brand as a hammer-wielding smasher of her opponents on the battlefield.

Your username appears in the Display Name window. From here, you can change upper- and lowercase and mix and match characters however you like. If your username consists of two or more words, consider formatting it in a way that's easy to read. For example, Burkeblack could be just initial capped, or camel case (also called medial capitals) can help folks read it as intended: BurkeBlack.

Bio

Your bio introduces you to people who want to learn more about your channel. Although some viewers chat and ask questions when you're live, most viewers tend to be lurkers, or people who watch without chatting. These viewers are more likely to watch for a short time and read your bio.

You get 300 characters to describe yourself in your bio. Although you want to be thorough, it's important to keep your bio short and easy to read. In fact, it can be good to get someone who knows you and your brand to help you create your bio. Remember, your bio is your best opportunity to let others know about the content you create.

It's worth mentioning that having a bio is a requirement for being discoverable to new users in the Twitch mobile app. Twitch attempts to help new users find channels they might like. To make this happen, Twitch asks its users what they like to watch and responds by displaying channels they might find interesting. The app displays only those channels that have bio descriptions, so lacking a bio can be detrimental to your growth.

Channel and Videos

The Channel and Videos section of the Settings page is all about adjusting how your viewers directly interact with you. From Content Settings to Banned Chatters, each section can be seen by the public. Some sections are relatively obscure unless they're brought to your attention; it's important to know what each section does.

Video Player Banner

The Video Player banner is the image that shows on your channel while you're offline. This image does not display if you're hosting another streamer, as their stream is overlaid where the banner normally appears. You can hide the hosted channel though, so it's still important to have a nice banner for anyone who visits your channel. The image you choose is entirely up to you, but many broadcasters follow a few common practices.

When you choose your Video Player banner, think about your brand and what you want potential viewers to see when they visit your channel for the first time. We delve into earning followers after a host or a raid later, but one major aspect of a platform-assisted raid is that it transfers all the chatters in a broadcaster's channel to the raid target's channel. Because most Twitch viewers are lurkers, they may be away from their computers during a raid, which means they might not know who you are. You need to provide some sort of introduction for when they return. Normally, your panels do this type of work, but sometimes lurkers don't return until after your stream ends—those viewers will come back to your Video Player banner, as long as you also didn't use the raid feature.

A Video Banner can also show your viewers when you're offline, where to follow you on other media, or when they can watch you live again. Some broadcasters use this space to display their streaming schedule, which is important information for anyone who follows your channel. Schedules have become much less prevalent with the introduction of interactive extensions, which can be used to count down the time to the next stream. This helps clear up confusion caused by time zones

Content Settings

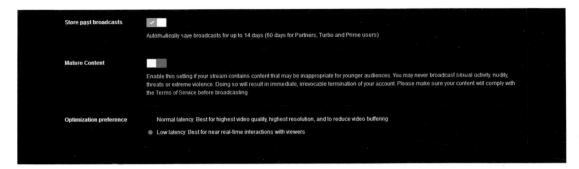

The Content Settings provides an age restriction toggle for your channel and its videos. Obviously, you aren't allowed to do anything prohibited by Twitch's Terms of Service, but this is where you can tell your audience whether your channel is "safe" to watch. You might use this option when young children are around, or if there's a chance mature language or content may arise during the stream. Just to be safe, it might be a good idea to keep the Mature Content setting toggled on. It will protect your audience from content that they may not want to see, and it will prevent your channel from getting suspended. A suspension can occur if you broadcast mature content when the setting is not toggled on, as you have failed to provide proper warning to viewers regarding the potentially offensive content. You can verbally warn your audience about mature content, but this is not adequate according to Twitch's Terms of Service.

Twitch doesn't permit users under 13 years of age to create an account, but you can expect some people to break this rule. Remember that you're obligated to ensure your content fits the settings you've chosen. Also, never ask for a viewer's age for this same reason. You don't want to be held accountable for broadcasting to someone who is breaking the rules of the platform. If someone claims that his or her age is below 13 (or 18 if the Mature Content setting toggled on), it's in your best interest to ban that viewer from your channel, at least temporarily, until they can prove they meet the age requirement—you will always be responsible for what happens in your channel. Often, broadcasters have a trusted moderator handle this responsibility; however, if the moderator makes a mistake, the broadcaster is still the person who is held accountable.

My Teams

Broadcasters have been trying to improve the Twitch teams feature since its creation. Team members can work together and utilize their audiences to expand their collective reach. Within My Teams, you can manage your preferences within your teams. You can accept team invitations here and adjust options that affect what the team owner sees and what your channel presents. Two check boxes allow the team owner of each team to see certain details about your channel. The Stats box, if checked, allows the team owner to see a basic report of your recent stream metrics. The Revenue box, if checked, allows the team owner to see the revenue you earned in recent streams. Keep in mind that you must be either an affiliate or a partner for the revenue option to be available. As the owner of your channel, you are not obligated to check either box since all of this is informational.

Lastly, you can select the "Main" bubble for only one team of which you are a member. You can join many teams, and you appear on each team's roster, but you can display only one team in your channel's team section; this is visible to the public. To reiterate, you appear in the rosters of all the teams you join, but only your "main" team appears in the spot where it says "team" on your channel. Clicking this bubble causes your channel to display the selected team.

Graveyard Keeper   Variety, UbiSF, VarietyStreaming   Illuminate

Chat Options

Site Description: **Moderate your channel's chat and who you allow in it.**

This section of the Channel and Videos tab is a little more complex. Chat Options allow you to regulate some of what happens in your channel's chat. As described by Twitch, this section can "moderate your channel's chat and who you allow in it." A few options located in "your dashboard" are customizable, allowing you to click through and/or shift to change your channel's settings. You'll spend time on the dashboard making adjustments on your channel, but most of it is straightforward, and the important aspects are explained further in this chapter's Your Dashboard section.

Block Hyperlinks

Site Description: **Your channel's chat will automatically delete posted URLs except for ones posted by you, moderators, and admins.**

In general, it's a good idea to block all hyperlinks posted in your channel's chat window, so we recommend clicking this option to its "on" position in the best interest of your chat. Most broadcasters use a third-party bot that will automatically timeout links posted in chat, as it's easier for the bot to regulate and let some links pass through a filter. Many broadcasters allow clips to be posted in their chat because clips tend to receive more clicks when they're posted immediately after the event. However, bots are completely optional in your chat. Bots are a great idea, especially to prevent malicious accounts from linking to inappropriate things. However, you can use Block Hyperlinks to protect those who like to click on links allowed in chat. It's good to turn on the Block Hyperlinks option while also using a bot that blocks hyperlinks. If you turn it off, just remember to make sure to use a bot and that it works properly.

Email Verification

Site Description: **Anyone who would like to send messages in your chat must first verify their email address.**

The email verification option has caused some issues for users in the past. However, it's usually good to turn it on as a secondary line of defense against malicious parties that quickly create new accounts just to cause headaches for broadcasters and their mods.

Chat Rules

Site Description: **Require first-time viewers to agree to your rules before chatting. One rule per line.**

Chat Rules allow you to post guidelines for your channel's chat. Using one rule per line, you can include multiple rules, but it's best to keep this section as brief as possible. Once you post your rules, when a new person enters your chat, a window stating the rules appears in the chat field. The viewer must click a button to agree to your rules in order to post in chat. This is a good way to ensure every chatter is prompted to read the rules—whether they do or don't is up to them. You have the option to timeout or ban a chatter for breaking your rules, a powerful tool for maintaining order in your channel's chat. Be sure to keep your rules as clear and simple as possible to avoid any confusion.

Non-Mod Chat Delay

Site Description: **Adds a short delay before non-mods see messages. Any message that is timed out or banned during the delay is removed from chat completely.**

If you're concerned about what is displayed in the chat window, explore the option called Non-Mod Chat Delay. Chat Delay is good for a few things, but it can also cause its own problems. As the description states, the chat will be live for the broadcaster and his or her mods. So, from your perspective nothing is different, and you can read posts as they are entered into chat. This allows you and your mods to delete messages before the public sees them, which is a real plus.

However, there are some negatives to discuss, which is why some broadcasters don't use the feature. Your chatters more than likely want to see everything when you see it. Watching the game and your reaction to it exactly as it happens, even with a delay, is understandable. However, it's a bit different when someone in chat types something and they don't immediately see it. Something about a delay can throw chatters off-kilter. There are options to adjust the time of the delay, so if you feel a delay is necessary but you also understand some viewers dislike it, you can always set the delay to two seconds, which is a great compromise. Spend some time in a channel with Non-Mod Chat Delay turned on to test it for yourself. See how you like being on the other side.

> *Quick Wisdom:* **If you don't have active mods who can continually monitor your chat, especially during a busy time, Non-Mod Chat Delay doesn't serve any purpose.**

Banned Chatters

To keep it simple, this section displays the usernames of those who have been banned from your channel, who banned each person, and the date on which he or she was banned. If anyone ever messages you after being banned and they don't understand why, this log is a good resource to help remind you of the reason.

Unfortunately, the Banned Chatters section gives you only the most basic information about the chatters who were banned. Often, that's all you really need, especially if you trust that your mods know exactly what they're doing and are looking out for your best interests. A few third-party tools gather a bit more information about banned chatters, or anyone who types something into your channel's chat. Almost every bot that exists tracks what's said in chat, but a popular one is called Logviewer (cbenni.com). This tool is extremely useful for a variety of reasons, but it works for tracking users you've banned on a deep level. cbenni's Logviewer tracks everything each user posts in your channel's chat, and the logs are fully searchable. This allows you to search for any user and read the transcripts of what they posted, which lets you decide whether the user's ban was appropriate. If it's important for you to keep a connection with those who reach out to you, as it can help strengthen your community, then use this tool to show banned users what they did wrong and possibly give them another chance.

Security and Privacy

Security

Password

This is where you can, and should, change your password—often. You've likely used websites that require passwords, so this is fairly straightforward. However, unlike most forums or media sites, you are a content creator, and the security of your account is important for your brand and livelihood. Developing a password or using a generator to regularly change your password can protect your channel from users who may want to take over your account.

Two-Factor Authentication

As one of the most important forms of security, everyone should turn on two-factor authentication. There are several ways malicious parties can access your password, especially if you use the same password on Twitch and other sites or accounts. Although you should never copy passwords, it does happen, and two-factor authentication is currently one of the best ways to protect your account. Even if someone obtains your password, in order to fully access your account, he or she will also need access to the device you use to authenticate a login.

Rule #1: Turn on Two-Factor Authentication. Please, do this.

Your Dashboard

Welcome to your dashboard... well, my dashboard, and specifically the Live section, as that's what we'll focus on within this section. The screenshot image probably looks similar to what you might find when you visit your dashboard. Remember, the dashboard is customizable, which means you can move each module around within the window. Your dashboard provides many helpful modules, though some are more important when your channel is live. So, arranging the modules to be readable at a glance while you're streaming is your best bet. Before you know which ones might be most important, let's quickly discuss each module.

Stream Information

Title

By far, this will be the most important module on your dashboard, as it's where you adjust the information your audience sees, as well as some of the categories in which your stream will appear when it's live. The title is at the top. You can add information here. You can make it say whatever you want as long as you abide by the Terms of Service. Popular streamers often use this section to give viewers basic information. You get only 140 characters, so keep it simple. Some use this section to tell their audience which game they're playing, because it's always good to provide this information in as many places as possible. If you're feeling creative, use it to write something that might attract viewers to your stream.

This is where it can get tricky—don't break any platform rules while you create a provocative title. Another common approach is to give your viewers information about the types of commands and information they can use in chat. Information commands allow a longer-form explanation about a given command; they also help draw attention to specific points that can prompt you, the broadcaster, to talk about on stream.

It's important to note that only the first 34 characters are visible to anyone who isn't in your channel. So, let's say your stream appears in someone's follow list, or perhaps someone is browsing the game you're playing and they look at your stream's thumbnail. That person will see the most current thumbnail from your livestream; the top-left corner of the thumbnail indicates whether it's a live broadcast or a rerun; and the top-right shows how long you've been live. More importantly, four items below the thumbnail are mostly under your control.

Your profile picture is among these items. Next, viewers see the title, followed by your name, and finally the name of the game you're playing. For this discussion, the important part is the title you create to represent your stream at a glance. This is should entice viewers to check out your stream, but remember you can use only 34 characters before an ellipsis appears, forcing folks to click on your stream to see the rest of the title. Therefore, creativity is key if you want to make someone click on that title.

Go Live Notification

Those who follow you are privy to additional information if they so choose. Your Go Live Notification is one example. As long as your followers have their live notifications turned on for your channel, the information will appear to those who are online. This notification appears in the top-right corner of the screen when one uses the browser version of the site, along with information from that window and a Watch or Close option. Naturally, those who click the Watch option go straight to your channel. Making this an enticing message, or simply something about the stream on that day, may prompt a viewer to click the Watch option, thereby boosting your viewer count.

Game/Category

This is where you list the game or category under which you're streaming. There are several alternatives to playing games on Twitch, which is why this option reads as such. Whatever you're doing on stream, make sure this information is accurate. Streaming too long under an incorrect category may cause problems, as it can confuse people and inadvertently make viewers feel you're dishonest. Unfortunately, once someone sees you as unprofessional, they may not give you a second chance.

Tags

This section is fairly new. Previously known as "communities," it was intended to serve as another listing for your stream (while you were live) to help viewers find channels in communities they enjoyed. It will eventually evolve into tags, because it becomes more about the individual broadcast and the general description of it rather than somewhat arbitrary communities. Using tags to describe your channel and place it in a section where you might find like-minded individuals can increase the focus in your community. The purpose is to help your discoverability, so being accurate with your tags can only help.

Language

The language section identifies the language you plan to use in your stream, as well as the language you prefer for chat. You don't need to use this section, but you should be accurate if you select the Restrict Chat Language option. Twitch has viewers all around the world, and most attempt to speak the language you do, but there are inherent problems with people who type out emoticon codes, which makes this system a little tough to use properly. It may be best to avoid using this option for the time being.

Host

The next module is the Host section. As we noted previously, hosting occurs when one broadcaster chooses to use the /host username function in their own chat to temporarily overlay the channel that he or she places in the "username" part of this command. This helps the channel you're hosting, as anyone watching your channel will now see the hosted channel's video as well. Fellow broadcasters can help each other by temporarily combining their communities.

This module provides the information about hosting as it pertains to your channel. The top section shows who you're hosting (if you happen to be hosting another channel), followed by who is hosting you, and who has you on their auto-host list. If you are not live, the "hosting you" section doesn't show anyone, as a host always drops off once a channel goes offline. When you're live, you can refer to this section for a live feed of the channels hosting your stream. The auto-host section displays those who have taken the extra effort to add you to their auto-host list.

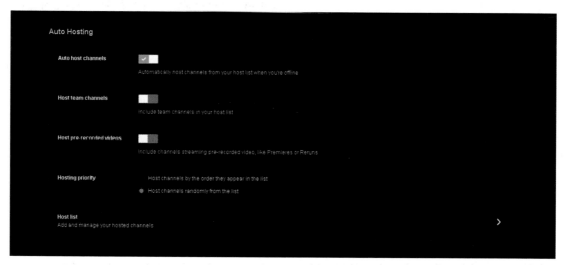

An auto-host occurs when a channel hosts your channel when you're live without that channel having to be live or able to host you manually under certain conditions. The conditions are listed in the screenshot. The important thing to know is that even though you may be live, you may not be hosted by the channels that have you on their auto-host list. You will not automatically gain an auto-host simply by being online. The channel must not be hosting someone else already. Furthermore, if the channel has someone ahead of you on their priority list, they will receive the auto-host first if they are live. Most channels don't get auto-hosted, but some do and it's important to acknowledge the channels that do this for you, as it's incredibly helpful to your channel.

Stream Health

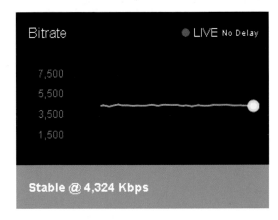

The Stream Health module is straightforward. It shows what your connection might be to the Twitch server you're using. This is a great module to watch if you're worried about your internet connection or your viewers comment about an unclear stream. If this is an issue, check out your streaming software. There's usually an area that shows your online status and the strength of your connection. If everything appears to be good, then check the Stream Health module. If the module displays an unstable connection, or if the graph is all over the place, then there's likely a connection issue of some sort.

Video Preview

The Video Preview module allows you to view the video that is being played to your channel without having to go to the channel itself. This module enables you to check on things if you don't trust the preview from your streaming software.

Stats

The Stats module displays the number of viewers, the amount of time you're live during a session, how many clips have been taken, your total live view count, your follower count, and—if you are a Twitch affiliate or a Twitch partner—the number of subscribers. This information isn't important while you're streaming, so don't let it distract you from what you're doing on stream unless you plan to celebrate a specific milestone.

For the most part, you can tell how well you're doing by gauging the entertainment level your viewers show in chat, so try to avoid thinking about it and instead focus on the stream.

Video Broadcast

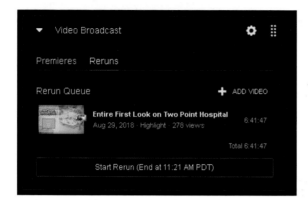

The Video Broadcast module contains a few features new to Twitch. One tab is the Premieres window, where you can schedule a premiere. A premiere is a video you reveal to your audience while you watch it live together. Think of it like a TV show that comes on at a certain time and viewers tune in for the premiere broadcast. Twitch will automatically start the video when you schedule it. You can't speak over the video, and nothing about it happens in real time, but you can use a premiere as a way to experience one of your creations with your audience.

The other tab is called Reruns. Reruns are videos of your previous streams. Like premieres, reruns play for everyone who is on your channel live. You can set any stream currently saved on your channel to rerun, and you can create a playlist to play as many different videos as you like, including highlights. Twitch does all the heavy lifting in this case; you can simply hang out in chat with your community, or not at all if you choose. Reruns are great for time slots that you may not normally be live, on vacation, sick, and so on.

Extensions

Extensions enhance a broadcast by adding interactive pieces to your channel. You can search for extensions to add to your channel on the extensions market, but understand that not every extension provides an option to manipulate it on your dashboard. Some extensions provide information to view on the fly, and if the designer adds the option to see it via your dashboard, that's where it will be. Some extensions, like Pretzel Rocks, which is one of our favorites, show the song that's playing on your stream. At the top of the Extensions module, you can switch to each extension and adjust it. However, you can see every extension you have installed in the extension marketplace, which is where you will do most of the configuration anyway.

Stream Markers

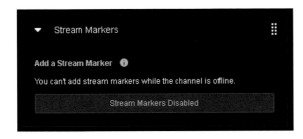

Stream Markers are also new to Twitch, and this may be one of the most important tools for broadcasters who like to highlight and mark certain points in a stream's video to help them piece together specific sections. If there's a point at which you change your game, or you finish a segment that you want to save and highlight, you can set a marker at any point in your broadcast. We encourage you to use this tool, because even if you don't have time or aren't comfortable highlighting or editing your past broadcasts, you may find a reason to go back in a broadcast and check out some of these marked points. There's no harm in marking your stream while it's live, and you can easily set a marker simply by typing /marker in your channel's chat.

Safety: Protecting Yourself and Your Community

The Most Important Chapter

This is perhaps one of the most important chapters in this book. Above all else, safety should be at the forefront of every broadcaster's mind. You really can't go too far when security is at stake, and many tools can protect you better than simply trying to conceal certain details live on your broadcast. Most broadcasters do a fine job hiding sensitive information while streaming, but your computer may hold data that you don't want to divulge inadvertently, which is why it's generally a bad idea to use monitor capture rather than game capture on your streaming software. Using a camera provides even more chances for something you don't want to share with your audience to show up on stream. You may take streaming seriously, but that doesn't mean folks around you or guests on your stream understand the platform well enough to respect your safety. Things can happen unexpectedly, possibly revealing privileged information. Make sure that, if your information happens to leak, you are still protected by a second line of defense. It's important to note that most people are not set on causing harm; instead, they just want to support your streaming career. As long as you're cautious and take the proper precautions, you shouldn't encounter any issues.

First Things First

Before we delve deeper into the importance of safety, we recommend you visit your local police station. Speak with an officer to let him or her know a little about what you do. In most states, as well as many countries outside the US, they will likely know what streaming is. As a broadcaster, you may be at greater risk than the average citizen of being targeted with false reports. Broadcasters have had their information stolen and used to "prank" or breach their privacy. The act of obtaining someone's personal information to share with malicious intent is known as "doxxing." Once someone possess this sensitive information, they may escalate to "swatting," in which case they alert the authorities to dispatch police to a place of residence. Of course, police are required to investigate any reports of suspicious activity. But with an open line of communication, they may better understand that you are not a threat, and they may be more cautious when responding to a potential call to your address.

Identity

Broadcasters and online influencers define their identities on the internet every day. Many details about a person's life comprise his or her identity, but often the more unique a person is, the more identifiable and unique his or her identity. In order for someone to be an identifiable streamer, people need to know about and like something about that person.

Creating a character can help protect sensitive parts of a broadcaster's identity. A characters provides an onscreen persona people can relate to and associate with the channel. It's easy to brand a character, as its creator can give it uniquely identifiable characteristics, such as behavior, appearance, or dialogue. However, a contrived persona can make it harder to be genuine with an audience without revealing something about the person behind the facade.

Another method to establish an identity without revealing too much information is to fully own your username—the name you use on Twitch. Before I started streaming on Twitch, I used the name Sabotage. Sabotage was an esports name born from tactics I used against opponents, so I became known for my play style and esports name. I owned the name and started leaning into it more and more. I played mind games with my opponents and the tools or traps they tried to use against me and my team. I made it my job to dismantle their strategy from back to front, rather than taking them head-on. My team was always good enough to hold the front lines, so there wasn't much stopping us from winning simply by following these tactics. However, this story isn't about my history as much as it is about how I made sure my identity was my brand.

For most of my time in competitive gaming, the public didn't know my first or last name. In a lot cases, no one saw my face. Esports were far different in the early 2000s, but the point is that this was a great way to create a brand and identity without giving away personal information.

Just remember, if you want to make a name for yourself in the streaming business, then people may focus on your real identity. Don't feel compelled to reveal too much personal information if it makes you uncomfortable. After all, it's your identity, so share only what you feel comfortable sharing with others.

Conventions

Conventions are some of the most useful events a broadcaster can attend to boost their career. Penny Arcade Expo (PAX), Rooster Teeth Expo (RTX), E3, Dreamhack, Insomnia, GamesCom, TwitchCon, and several others are fantastic venues for expanding your channel's reach. I've met some of my closest friends at conventions and chatted for hours about the industry or introduced each other to folks in our own circles.

It's relatively safe to participate in conventions, but it's wise to take a few precautions because lots of people are in attendance. Many broadcasters don't realize they enter a spotlight when they start to gain success and popularity, and losing a bit of privacy comes with the territory. Some people who want your attention may, to a greater or lesser degree, breach your privacy to get it. While some are happy to wait for a tweet to find out where to meet you, others may decide to seek you out, even if they have the best intentions. Gamers are generally lovely people—they're often more respectful than the average person.

Words of Wisdom

In preparation for this book, I sat down with Omeed Dariani, the CEO of a talent management group called Online Performers Group, or OPG. In the interest of full disclosure, I should mention that Omeed and the Online Performers Group manage and represent me, Danotage. This is how I knew I'd receive the wisdom I did during my conversation with him. Omeed knows a lot about the industry. In fact, you may have read a few of his tweets (@Omeed) about broadcasters, sponsors, and the Twitch community as a whole.

We've sprinkled some of this wisdom throughout this book. What was most important, though, was the information he revealed when I asked, "What are some of your most important goals when you attend a convention?" Before I could finish the question, the first word out of his mouth was "safety." Enough incidents have occurred at conventions that safety should be at the forefront of everyone's mind. He went on to talk about how the first thing he does at a convention is to make sure that, once everyone under his watch has arrived, they are set up and have everything they need. There have been many attempts to harm broadcasters, so taking the time to keep everyone safe is a priority for the OP Group.

Traveling with a companion is always a good idea, and conventions are no different. Even if the convention is local, it's wise to attend with a trusted friend by your side. This also applies to late-night and after-hours events during conventions. Late dinners and parties are common. Although most people behave responsibly at these activities, there's always a chance you'll encounter a problematic person looking to exploit those who let down their guard or overindulge in alcohol.

All in All

If you plan to make a career of broadcasting, it's important to know you stand a slightly higher chance of being cyber-attacked than most internet users. However, being respectful of your followers and other broadcasters greatly reduces that risk. Always use two-factor authentication for everything you access online, especially if it's connected to your streaming persona or something that might appear on your stream. Protect yourself and your identity as much as possible. Sometimes this means keeping everything secret—you have to choose whether you want people to know your true identity in addition to your username. I don't recommend revealing much more than your first name, but if you must, I suggest removing your residential address from public record so it's less accessible. You can do this by contacting The White Pages or any other business that lists this information and politely explaining your situation.

The same idea applies to gaming with your friends and community in multiplayer games that don't hide your PC's IP address. Research the multiplayer options for games your community may join in a session. Many games do a great job keeping users relatively anonymous, but other games require players to connect to each other via IP address. If this is the case, it's best to play only with people you trust or no one at all. You may also want to create a private server with either a first- or third-party that has IP protection. As always, you should have the most up-to-date network security on your PC.

Tools and Features

Livestreaming is a booming activity and growing industry. There are hundreds of thousands of channels, each with its own unique characteristics, qualities, communities, and livestreamer personalities. It can be daunting to enter a space that has so many options and opportunities—where do you start?

As livestreaming has gained popularity over the years, individuals and companies have created new tools and programs to enhance the stream experience for both the broadcaster and viewer. It's now easier than ever to find programs that help you, the broadcaster, make the kind of content you want. Additionally, Twitch has continued to expand the platform's standard features to facilitate new streamers, affiliates, and partners.

Let's take a look at some tools and features Twitch provides to help get your channel started on the right foot.

Twitch Chat and the Tools to Use

The chat feature is the most beloved and well-used feature on Twitch. It revolutionized the interactive entertainment medium, and it's what brought such success to Twitch in the early years. It is the avenue by which viewers talk with livestreamers and each other, and it adds a layer of interactivity and connectivity that other mediums lack. It can be a channel's defining characteristic, or it can be an afterthought where viewers chat only when necessary. Regardless of how it is used, the Twitch chat feature is a component of every livestream channel.

If you are new to livestreaming, it's important for you to learn as much as you can about the chat feature set to see how you can utilize it on your channel.

On your channel page, you can find the chat box on the right-hand side. Anyone looking at your channel can see the chat box and read its contents. However, a person must be logged into a Twitch account in order to send messages in chat.

Understanding that the chat feature is a big reason why viewers watch livestreams, Twitch supports the feature by allowing access to internal and external development. This has opened the way for many different systems and tools to interact with chat, and Twitch will continue to enhance chat features for years to come. Let's look at some of the specifics of Twitch chat: badges, emoticons, commands, and bots.

Badges

Badges are small icons that appear before a username in Twitch chat. They're reserved for important information that's intended to stand out to the viewers in chat; these icons can help denote user roles, such as admin, moderator, or streamer (the owner of the channel).

   As Twitch continues to expand chat functionality, the number of badges available in chat has increased. Streamers can now reward their longtime subscribers with unique, channel-only subscription badges. Attendees of TwitchCon events can have their unique TwitchCon badges displayed in all Twitch chats. Twitch Turbo and Twitch Prime users can also display their unique badges in all Twitch chats.

Badges can be compelling incentives for viewers. They can remind viewers to strive for achievements within the channels they watch, and they can be fun to celebrate when viewers reach these milestones. As a Twitch broadcaster, think about what your subscriber badges will look like. This should tie in closely with the branding you choose for your channel, which is discussed in a later chapter of this book.

Emoticons

Emoticons, or emotes, are unique images that display in Twitch chat. They convey a message or emotion via an image, instead of using text. Mostly, they offer a fun way for viewers to message and interact with each other and the streamer. For example, a viewer who just joined the channel could use an emote of someone waving their hand in chat instead of typing out "hello." Emoticons provide a dynamic, ever-changing, and fundamental feature that can help bring your chat to life.

The emoticon feature can be used by anyone in chat, but not all emotes are available to everyone. Some emotes have specific prerequisites in order for the viewer to be able to use them in chat. You can see which emotes are available to you by clicking on the happy face icon in the chat message box.

Let's break down these emotes into two types: global and unique.

Twitch provides global emoticons, and they are usable on all channels by any viewer. Although many global emotes are permanent, Twitch periodically updates and adds new global emotes for special or current events. You can see the full list on Help.Twitch.TV, or by clicking on the happy face icon in the chat message window in Twitch chat.

Unique emoticons are those that Twitch does not create internally, and they are not available to everyone. They are created by artists and streamers for their specific livestream channels, meaning they represent the streamer's or the channel's brand. They often need to be unlocked before a viewer can use them in chat. Unique emotes are externally created and uploaded to Twitch, and can be updated at any time by the streamer. Twitch reserves the right to review and approve all emotes, and this review process can take a number of days. Unique emotes are usable across all Twitch channels, but the criteria for gaining access to them must first be fulfilled on the specific Twitch channel where they are created and uploaded.

TIP: To reiterate, unique emotes are specific to the channel—the streamer creates and uploads the emotes. They convey messages or branding for that channel, and once a viewer has access to the emotes, he or she can use them in any Twitch chat globally.

Twitch offers different levels of unique emotes for affiliates and partners. Affiliates are offered three emote slots, one for each subscription tier. This means that if someone subscribes to an affiliate for Tier 1 (the lowest-price subscription), then the Tier 1 emote on that channel will become available to the viewer for use in chat. Similarly, if someone subscribes to that same affiliate for Tier 3 (highest-price subscription), then emotes for Tiers 1, 2, and 3 become available for that viewer to use in chat.

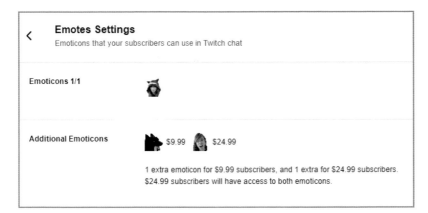

Twitch partners begin with a handful of emote slots, and are offered up to 50 emote slots total. The number of emotes available for a partner depends on the number of subscriber points they have. Each subscription tier is worth a set number of points (Tier 1 = 1 point, Tier 2 = 2 points, Tier 3 = 3 points), and new emote slots are unlocked as the Partner's subscription points accumulate. The current level is 50 emote slots for 7,000 subscriber points.

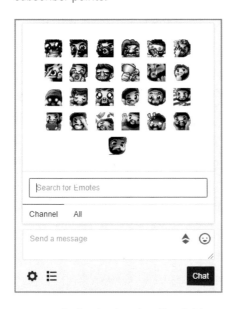

Emotes are a highly coveted feature in Twitch chat. Affiliates and partners alike create compelling and unique emotes for their channels to entice and reward viewers for subscribing. Each emote has a unique code name which one can type into chat to display the emote, or one can click on the happy face icon in the message box to see all the available emotes.

LIVESTREAMER INTERVIEW: SirSlaw (Twitch.tv/SirSlaw)

Q: Can you describe what you think makes a compelling emote?

A: I come from a background of software design, but before that I practiced product design and trying to develop the right user experience. I always try to make things people want to come back to. So, when it comes to designing my emotes, I'm very particular about the artist I bring on board.

Emotes can trigger an emotion or a feeling, very much like emoji in text messaging. They convey messages that are a little more difficult, or subtle, to convey in words. They also sort of capitalize on a cultural movement within Twitch itself.

In my opinion, emotes that stand out are ones that touch on cultural landmarks. Alternatively, some emotes create cultural landmarks of their own. For example, if one channel's emotes become so pervasive that other channels create emotes and memes off of them, then that's the best example of creating something powerful.

Q: What do you think about when you create and define subscriber badges versus subscriber emotes?

A: I feel like I come from a pretty unique place and perspective, less from my own brand and channel—the fact is, I'm really new to livestreaming. I've only been doing this for about a year. I don't have nearly as much personal, firsthand experience, so a lot of this is guess work, gut feeling, and intuition. It's a lot of experimentation.

I feel like a lot of people make emotes that fit their channel's brand or the things they want to put out there. Right now, I'm just having fun with it. I'm creating things that I think are cute or can spark their own cultural movements within Twitch.

When I was getting my emotes designed, the first thing I looked for was an artist that was exclusive. I wanted an artist with a pretty unique style and would be easy to differentiate from other emote styles. Something very legible and easy to see in chat. Those were really the only criteria for me—I just wanted to stand out, but I didn't have any designs in mind. The emotes I choose to create were fairly generic, like "hype" and "love," the stuff that everybody has.

However, when I first started streaming and became an affiliate, I didn't have an artist at the time. I had to design my own emotes, so I looked back at moments in my life, things that were relevant to Twitch culture, and I tried to project what I thought would be relevant to Twitch culture in the future. So, I made a "words are hard" emote—we've all had that moment in livestreaming when we flub over words, and the viewers say, "ha-ha, you messed up, man!" And that became this mantra in my channel. It then became a mission, with this "SirsWords" emote, that the channel was going to make this a global emote, and it has since taken over the channel. Every day for the past year, we always talk about it. So, that's an example of using something really prominent in your life, especially if it's something true to you, that people can latch onto.

LIVESTREAMER INTERVIEW: TehMorag (Twitch.tv/TehMorag)

Q: Can you describe what you think makes a compelling emote?

A: We're seeing this structure right now on Twitch, where the emote itself is being bought because of what the emote is. You're going to have communities were the emotes are memes for that community; you're going to have emotes that just fit the niche crowd of that community. But then you're also going to have emotes that literally sell themselves. The biggest thing right now is the cute, super fluffy anime-style emotes. So, what's the essence of it? I'd say to define whatever your aim is for your emotes. If you want to make emotes for your community, make them about your community. Give the community what they want. If you want to sell emotes, then see what the current meme and niche emotes are like and follow those. If you want to try to push a new meme in your own community, now you have an avenue for that.

I have people who buy my emotes and they're not even part of my community, so I know that they sell, and I try to find ways to push that if I can.

Q: What do you think about when you create and define subscriber badges versus subscriber emotes?

A: That, by itself, is something I've been battling and wrestling with. More than anything, I'm wrestling with my branding. What defines me? Who am I? What's the easiest way to define me and my reason for doing it in image form? Through the sub badges and emotes and memes, how you wish to be seen in an instant snapshot.

An emote is nice, but it's always nice seeing a person's face. An emote is an example of a person. It's a representative of who you are. But seeing someone face-to-face; they aren't an emote, they're a human being. So, it's trying to find that combination: your uniqueness with your branding to push who you are. It's tough. It's the puzzle that can never be solved. And if you figure it out, and some people have... Oh, I envy you.

Q: What do you think of platform-wide memes for emotes, like W emotes?

A: W emotes, if I remember correctly, originated as a wall emote. It was a square box, and it came from another big-name streamer. Then someone else made the first noseless one, and they ended up making a whole bunch for a lot of different streamers. Then we just had attack of the noseless wall face emotes.

It's still by far my favorite emote in my set, my community loves it, and it's my most used emote to this day. It ends up portraying sarcasm, in jest, light humor—Kappa but without the connotation of negativity that comes with that sometimes. It's interesting, it's multi-faceted. Is that a part of who I am? It is now because it was part of the meme, it grew on me, my community loved it, and now it's something that if I were to take it away, it would create a type of distrust at that point.

This is especially true if you start building your community upon memes and memes and memes, and then you start pulling some of those out from underneath your community's rug. If you're not careful, they will remember that forever.

Q: When a meme spreads throughout an entire community, do you think that builds camaraderie?

A: Oh, I'd definitely say so. It adds that extra layer, a representative of the community as a whole. The funny thing is, even though we see this as a good camaraderie link, what we don't see are the people who are not happy with it. The ones who are indifferent or really hate it. But as the platform grows, broadcasters start to self-sabotage a little bit. You start seeing more of that counteract what you're doing, and you feel that you need to change to accommodate other people.

It creates camaraderie, but over time and across age people get different ideas about what camaraderie is. Another example of a meme that has spread through the platform is calling the chat "chat." I've seen discussions on social media about this, where someone felt that the term was impersonal and they wanted to be called by their name, or for the caster to just use a term like "everybody." So, just a few more examples of memes that work for camaraderie and ones that don't. And this starts to go back to your brand, who you are, and how you want to describe your community.

Commands

Commands are lines of text that you type into chat to tell the system to do a specific thing. Commands are meant to be short and simple for ease of use. Some commands can be used by everyone, while other commands are used only by specific user types (e.g., streamer-only commands vs. viewer commands).

Example of a command:
A streamer can type /slow in chat to slow down the speed at which chat messages appear in the chat box. This can be a great way to read and catch a lot of the messages being sent in chat if you have a lot of viewers sending messages at once.

Twitch has a number of standard commands, which can be referenced on the Help.Twitch.TV website. Twitch commands always start with "/" (without the quotation marks) at the beginning of the message. Basic commands for all users include seeing a list of moderator accounts in the channel (**/mods**), ignoring or "un-ignoring" other viewers in chat (**/ignore <name>**, **/unignore <name>**), and disconnecting from the chat (**/disconnect**).

All livestreamers and moderators should be familiar with some basic streamer commands, including how to timeout or ban (i.e., forever remove) users from their chat (**/timeout <name>**, **/ban <name>**), slow down the chat message display speed (**/slow**), and clear the chat messages and history (**/clear**). These powerful commands can shape the experience of your viewers. It's especially important to watch for problematic chat users who try to make the experience uncomfortable for other viewers and the streamer. These commands can help remove unwanted messages, and timeouts and bans can set examples for the types of chat messages that will and won't be allowed on your channel.

Streamers can also use commands to host (**/host <name>**) or unhost (**/unhost <name>**) content on other channels while the streamer is offline. This can be a great way to support other broadcasters and provide your viewers with continuing content before and after your livestreams.

One of the most important and powerful commands a streamer can use is the mod command, which allows the streamer to "mod" viewers in chat (**/mod <name>**). The command stands for moderator, and the role is coveted across Twitch channels. If a viewer is modded, it means that person can use select streamer commands, such as **/timeout**, **/ban**, and **/slow**. Moderators are meant to help a streamer control the messages and content displayed in chat, and they can be your first line of defense against unwanted or inappropriate content.

In Twitch's early years, some broadcasters concluded their livestreams by finding another channel and "raiding" it. While the process was informal in the past, Twitch has now created a command that officially supports raiding on the platform. A raid consists of finding a channel that's currently live and sending your viewers there to continue watching that streamer's broadcast after you end your stream. By typing the raid command (**/raid <name>**) into chat, you begin a countdown timer that all viewers can see in your chat window. You then have a limited amount of time to say parting words to your viewers before your stream automatically turns off and you auto-host the channel you targeted with the raid. It's common to encourage your viewers to follow the new channel and have them say a particular catchphrase or "raid call" in the new channel's chat. The streamer that's being raided will get a notification, and he or she will usually welcome the new viewers to the channel. The objective of raiding is to support new content and streamers by hosting their feeds on other channels and sending viewers to a channel that they may not have discovered.

 TIP: Some streamers prefer to turn off raids in their channels, as a large influx of new viewers and chatters can disrupt the streamers' discussions or content creation. By and large, raiding is an understood and accepted practice on Twitch.

Viewers can directly support streamers via the Cheer command, which gifts the streamer monetary "Bits." This command doesn't display like other commands in the strictest sense; you do not need to include a "/" before the command word for the command to register in the chat window. By typing "cheerXXX" (XXX being a number from 1 to 10000), you initiate the Cheer Chat pop-up window where you can select an emote and a written text message to display with the gifted Bits. Each Bit equates to 1 cent, and you can purchase Bits by clicking on the Get Bits button in the chat window. When a viewer sends a streamer Bits via the Cheer command, they will automatically get a Cheer Badge added to the beginning of their name in chat. There are many different Cheer Badges, ranging from a 1 Bit Badge to a 1,000,000 Bit Badge, and each livestreamer has the ability to tailor which Bit Badges display in their channels and what minimum and maximum Bit values are supported via the Cheer command.

Outside of the standard commands and chat features, Twitch also provides methods for external developers to create their own commands. These commands are channel-specific and must be created or enabled by the livestreamer in a separate program, usually called a "bot." A standard practice for livestreamers is to find bots that have features they like, and then enable those bots on their channels to run custom commands (custom commands begin with "!" instead of "/"). We dive into more details on bots and their benefits in the Third Party Tools and Features section.

LIVESTREAMER INTERVIEW: SirSlaw (Twitch.tv/SirSlaw)

Q: What commands do you think are most helpful to viewers?

A: The commands I find the most valuable for viewers aren't the standard ones most broadcasters use. I, of course, use commands and track their usefulness or their engagement, things like !giveaway or special commands that provide more information on the game I'm playing. A lot of broadcasters do these, and they provide some value to very specific viewers. However, my personal favorite commands that provide the most value for viewers are those that allow them to interact with each other.

For example, I was streaming and asked viewers how their days were. Someone in chat responded, saying "Okay, I just got out of the shower. How is the stream?" and I immediately asked, "How was your shower?" And, of course, chat got on me about that. Obviously, because that's creepy. And one of the mods made that a command in chat, so now whenever you type !greet <viewer name> in chat, it will say "Greetings (viewer name)! How was your shower?" So, in particular, the commands that tag other viewers make people feel included. I'm all about inclusion and engagement, things that are interactive, that's what I'm all about.

LIVESTREAMER INTERVIEW: TehMorag (Twitch.tv/TehMorag)

Q: What are some of your favorite commands?

A: I've always enjoyed the weather command, to be honest. It's not just there to pick up the weather for yourself. When you do this command, a person voluntarily gives up a location. I don't mean this in a creepy way, but they're giving up a little bit more about themselves. It's imparted on the rest of the community. They get to understand how far people end up coming, being around the world, into this community you have. It's the one reason I've never disabled it.

I use three different chat bots in my channel. One is for the weather and back end moderation for caps lock and spam, another for giveaways and song requests, and then I have my own bot for points, quotes, my own custom commands, and my timers. It's all highly customized to what I do.

Q: What commands do you think are most helpful to viewers?

A: I have a time command, a caster command, shout outs commands to people's channels, a game command that displays what game I'm playing, and a URL to a purchase page. Some commands will be based around the games you're currently playing. Like if you're running any type of mods on your game, include a list of mods that you're showing in-game in chat, or link to a shared document with that information. If you're playing on a server, create a command to let viewers know what server you're on. Create commands to say "sorry, this is single-player," or "sorry, this is sub-only." Stuff that very much pertains to the game you're currently playing or are always interested in.

Try to interlink yourself to other, external communities as well. So, if there's a website that has heavy community influence on the game you're playing, include links to that as well.

The tools you provide can be used by your moderators and viewers. Some broadcasters limit their commands to subs or moderators only. I've had issues in the past of people spamming commands. At least for me, what I have is a page dedicated to commands. If you want to read them, look for them there. You don't need to put the command list in chat. And if someone starts spamming the commands, time them out.

Q: What do you think about adding commands that answer frequently asked questions from chat?

A: This really comes down to the broadcaster and how they communicate with their community. Depending on the caster and how they want to show themselves, you're going to have high skill cap players that are not going to talk to their chat a whole lot. They might talk here and there, but the main reason people are there is for the broadcaster's game skill. What's funny is that you're still going to come across people that say different things about different levels of interactivity. Someone is going to come into one channel and determine that the caster isn't interactive enough, and then go to another caster that talks all the time and say, "This person is interactive." But another person will go to that same talkative streamer and say, "This person is not interactive because I didn't get answered." There's no way to beat this, so what do you end up doing? You set up the tools to allow your community to answer questions.

If you have a command for literally every little thing, that can be too much. Instead of individual commands, have a link to a shared document or a channel layout with lots of information in it. Speedrunners use this technique. The good streaming speedrunners can explain things as they play, but most speedrunners set up nice, long FAQ docs. In some way, just get the information out there. If you know you're not talking a lot on stream, set up the FAQ. If you don't have the FAQ, then you'd better be talking a lot because you need to find a way to communicate and provide this information to your community.

Extensions

With the expanding development of integrated apps, some bot functionality is being integrated directly into Twitch via extensions. For instance, if a streamer wants to display her stream schedule, then she can use a bot to create a custom command, like !schedule, for viewers to use in chat to display a text version of the schedule. Or, she can add an extension that displays her stream schedule in the panels section of the channel below the live feed... or both! You can find out more about integrated functionality in the Panel Information and Extensions section of this book.

LIVESTREAMER INTERVIEW: TehMorag (Twitch.tv/TehMorag)

Q: What do you think of extensions, and do you use any on your channel?

A: I've been lazy, and I haven't looked at any myself. I end up playing a multitude of different games, so I haven't stuck to one game where a game extension would work to have that information readily available.

As for being an overall community-building tool, that's a tough one. I haven't really seen anything new or big that I would want to add to my community right now. It really depends on the extension itself. Don't get me wrong, extensions are fantastic. I just haven't found ones that fit my community.

LIVESTREAMER INTERVIEW: SirSlaw (Twitch.tv/SirSlaw)

Q: What do you think constitutes a good extension (for you, for your viewers, etc.)?

A: At the end of the day, extensions need to provide more value to people. Seeing leaderboards is fine and dandy, seeing a schedule in an extension is valuable and can help, but these extensions take up valuable screen real estate. In terms of extensions that provide value to communities, I want to see extensions that answer questions for people or help a broadcaster do his or her job in some way. A common example is if a viewer asks the broadcaster what they think about the game they're currently playing. The broadcaster answers this question all the time, multiple times per stream. So, why not have an extension that sums this up for the viewer instead? Or something that allows viewers to say whether they like the game the broadcaster is playing. In the end, extensions should provide more value over time.

LIVESTREAM INTERVIEW: missharvey (Twitch.tv/missharvey)

Q: Do you use extensions on your Twitch channel?

A: Yes, I do! I use a loyalty extension with an onscreen overlay. It's a little confusing for viewers, so I don't think it's very effective. I have my custom emotes added in the extension as well, so when you see an egg onscreen—because I have chickens as my team brand—you can click on the egg to find out more information.

I also use an extension for people to vote on things, and they can win custom currency through the extension. Not everyone uses it, but it's an option for my community.

Moderator Features

As mentioned in this chapter's Badges and Commands sections, a moderator, or "mod," is a viewer that has been given administrative rights within a specific Twitch channel. A mod user will display the unique moderator badge in the chat, but only in the channel where he or she has been upgraded to a moderator position. This badge indicates to other viewers that the user is a trusted member of the stream channel, and has the power to timeout and ban other members of chat.

TIP: A streamer can mod any number of viewers in his or her channel. However, we recommend limiting the number of mods to only those who are available and willing to help manage the channel during the livestream schedule.

Mods are extremely helpful during a livestream. They provide timely information and answer questions for viewers in chat, and monitor messages while the streamer focuses on creating content. It's important to keep in mind that moderators are people and should be treated with respect and kindness at all times. They usually mod the channel for no monetary gain or benefit, except to see the livestream succeed. In rare situations, mods can be paid for their work, but that is limited to agreements between the streamer and moderator. Twitch does not offer moderator payment or employment on individual Twitch channels.

Moderators are vital to livestream channels, and every major livestreamer has mod support. One hears it often from full-time streamers—their mods are essential to their administrative management, and they often praise and support their mods however they can. We recommend you provide your mods with the tools and support they need to help manage your channel. Setting up regular meetings with your moderators to discuss schedule changes, what games to play, and upcoming special events can keep everyone in line with the content you want to make and how to promote and support that content when the time is right.

Global mods are users who have mod privileges across all Twitch livestream channels. They are volunteers approved by Twitch to provide support and advice to all viewers and streamers.

Moderators: Twitch Features

A moderator of a channel has access to Twitch chat commands that are not available to normal viewers.

These powerful commands can sway the course of the chat, including limiting chat messages to channel followers or subscribers only. Mods can slow down the chat when there is an influx of new messages, and can timeout and ban problematic viewers. Outside of the Twitch chat, moderators can also be added as "editors" to Twitch livestream channels.

In the Settings - Permissions section of your Twitch dashboard, you can add editors to your channel. Editors can manage and edit certain parts of the livestream channel, including the game information (what game the streamer is currently playing), uploading videos to the Video Producer section, and creating events that can be promoted and shared with a community. Editors don't have to be moderators in your channel, but it can help to give some of your mods access to your channel as editors to make on-the-fly channel edits before and during your livestream, as well as create post-stream clips and video updates.

Moderators: Tools

Streamers can allow moderators to use custom commands in Twitch chat via an external bot. These commands can range from triggering informational messages to allowing viewers to post links in chat. The bot features for moderators vary per application, and can provide an impressive range of control when maximized.

In the end, all the additional tools and features mean little if the moderators themselves aren't in line with the streamer. The most important things to keep in mind are to be selective with whom you mod, and set up good communication processes with the mods in your channel. If you have a solid foundation of moderators and have established good communication and practices with your mod team, then you're already on your way to a successful Twitch channel.

LIVESTREAMER INTERVIEW: TehMorag (Twitch.tv/TehMorag)

Q: What is important for livestreamers to think about regarding their moderators?

A: You do not need to have a moderator to have a successful stream. If you end up feeling overburdened or overrun, you might blame your moderators. Or, if you're a new streamer and you're trying to build up your channel and you mod someone, then you may still feel overwhelmed with work, and you may blame yourself and use them as a scapegoat.

You should use moderators to highlight leaders in the community. They are examples of great community members. That's what I personally use my moderators as. If a person asks a question, my moderator is the first to answer their question, and tags them in the response. If someone asks about the game, the moderator will use the !game command and will tag the person as well.

Q: Are certain people important to your community, but you don't give them moderator permissions?

A: This is an interesting topic, because it's asking does longevity in your community determine worth and the trust of "mod-ship?" This is one argument that some people raise, or some casters even use for who gets to be moderators in their channel. Yes, there will definitely be people in the community that just don't fit the moderator role, even though they've been there for a very long time. Does it have to do with them being just a little bit edgier, or how they respond to people in the chat? One feature I look for in my mods is not to have a combative attitude. What I mean by that is, if someone puts a weird comment in chat, and then someone else is defensive about it, then the mods need to be unbiased, deal with it, and move on.

Do your friends become moderators? It's something to be careful with. Your moderators are your community, and sometimes your friends aren't always going to be there, and people in chat won't know that. All they see is the badge next to their name. Sometimes your friends may act in a way that isn't what your stream is about, so be careful. Let your friends know what type of attitude you're trying to show within the community.

LIVESTREAMER INTERVIEW: LittleSiha (Twitch.tv/LittleSiha)

Q: What's important for livestreamers to think about regarding their moderators?

A: A huge mistake I personally think a lot of newer streamers make is moderating users just because they're very generous with their money by tipping a lot, or being big sub gifters. I really believe it comes from a place of gratitude and wanting to repay folks for all they've given us. But if that's the only reason for giving someone power in your channel, it can be dangerous. My number one rule about modding a user is determining whether I can see myself being friends with them outside of Twitch. If I've known them for a long time, if I believe they have good judgement and are responsible, I absolutely trust them with power in my channel. I view my channel as my baby; if I'm going to let someone babysit it, I need to know that they're responsible.

LIVESTREAMER INTERVIEW: Venalis (Twitch.tv/Venalis)

Q: What's important for livestreamers to think about regarding their moderators?

A: Firstly, never moderate anyone who asks for it. Ever.

There are two key things to look for in moderators: the first is try to find a person who is already acting like a moderator. They don't have the sword badge, you've never hinted to them that you're looking for a moderator; they just naturally answer questions from other viewers about what the streamer is doing, their progress in the game, and links to the stream schedule and information. Always look for that viewer who is already acting like a moderator.

Secondly, do not moderate your friends for the sake of friendship. It usually goes down a really weird avenue. Moderate people who could also have a job. For instance, I have moderators in my crew who are "welcome bots." They are the chatters and they welcome people in chat, and they keep discussions going 24/7. Then I have my technical mods: the guy who runs the animations on my channel, the guy who runs the coding on all my sites. I even have a Reddit guru mod. Then, typically, you have a lead mod who organizes the crew. In essence, moderate for a purpose.

Every single streamer that has ever "made it" on Twitch had an amazing moderator team. And that's not speculation; that's me asking many streamers for advice about this exact topic.

Q: How do you handle your time and working with your moderator team? Are there limits that you put in place for their work and time?

A: There are many different methods for this. For me, I'm a free-for-all. If the moderators have something they want to bring to me, my DMs are always open. I try to schedule two mod meetings a month to go over plans, games they've heard of that I haven't, ask questions here and there.

All moderators work for free. The hope for every streamer is to get big enough to say "thank you" to their mods monetarily. Personally, I'm not even at the point where I can do that yet. What I do is set aside a little money here and there each month, and twice a year for the big PC game sales, I go through my moderator's wish lists and buy all the games for them. It's just a little something for my team of six or seven moderators, and it's something I like to do. I'd like to someday get to the point where I can hire moderators as paid employees of the LLC.

Twitch Communities

Twitch Communities offer another way to categorize content and find similar streamers on Twitch. Located under the Browse section of Twitch, viewers can sort livestreams by Communities, which displays live channels that adhere to a particular set of rules and guidelines. Twitch users (streamers or viewers) can create Communities, and they must contain Community Rules, adhere to the Twitch Terms of Service, and respect the official Community Guidelines.

Livestreamers can add up to three Communities to their channel. Adding Communities is like adding a category or label to your channel, wherein your stream will display under those Community categories on Twitch once you go live. You can update, add, or remove Communities from your channel at any time.

Game Communities

Communities centered around specific games are located under the Browse - Communities section on Twitch. Most Game Communities require that the streamer play only that game while using the specific Community tag, but some Communities allow for a variety of streams as well. Game Communities are a great way for viewers to find streams of a particular game they are interested in, and they can help streamers broaden their reach and viewership. Variety streamers can add the Communities relevant to the game they're currently playing in order to appear in searches for those Communities.

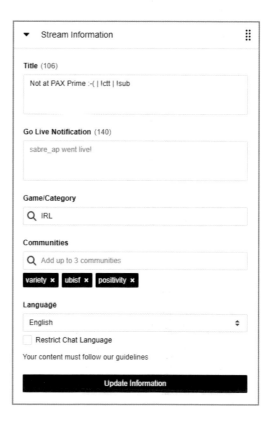

Creative Communities

Creative streams, which continue to grow in popularity on Twitch, focus on product creation instead of gaming content. Creative streams can be anything from the creation and exploration of music and artwork to food and cosplay. Some common categories defined as Creative include IRL (in real life), music, comedy, painting, drawing, food, cosplay, and game development to name just a few. Streamers can join Creative Communities to support their craft and find viewers interested in seeing their specific types of content.

Theme Communities

Perhaps a more abstract take on Communities are themes that revolve around a purpose, the love of a shared genre, or an idea rather than specific content. You can find these Communities under either the Browse - Communities or Browse - Creative Communities filters. Just a few examples include relaxation, positivity, and "Bearded Bros" (the last one involving a love of beards, as you might imagine).

As you become accustomed to streaming and better define the type of content you want to make, joining Communities on Twitch can be a great way for your channel to get discovered. Continue to experiment and join different Communities to see what works best for your channel.

Upcoming Changes to Communities

As Twitch continues to expand and refine its tools for finding content and streamers, you'll continue to see changes in the ways livestreamers can categorize their broadcasts. One such change will be the adaptation of keywords, or tags, for broadcasters to use on their channels. These tags may be added to supplement Communities, or they may replace Communities altogether. The underlying principle should remain consistent, and tags should be utilized for viewers to find streamers who provide the content that they find interesting and relevant.

The types of Communities and tags that Twitch supports will continue to evolve, so keep checking to see what's new and which ones you can use to best support your content. And remember, you can always try making a Community of your own!

Common Etiquette

Interacting with Viewers

Viewer and streamer interaction is a monumentally important part of livestreaming on Twitch. If you ask Twitch viewers why they watch livestreams, many will say the real-time streamer interaction with chat is an enticing draw. Chat interaction isn't always needed for the type of channel or content you create, but it never hurts for a streamer to interact with viewers in chat. This includes responding to chat messages, statements, and questions from viewers. Simply saying "hi" when someone types "hello" to you in chat can make a big difference in the viewer's experience.

As you define your channel and build your brand, you need to determine what kind of personality to portray on your stream. You don't need to take on a completely new persona or act differently than you normally would with people face-to-face. But understanding how you interact with people and what works best for you can help determine how you approach streaming, and it can set expectations for yourself and your viewers.

Some streamers are adept at keeping the conversation going. It can come naturally to some and be a struggle for others. It may be enough for you to interact with chat by having stream-of-conscious discussions about the game, telling stories, or saying anything that comes to mind. On the other hand, you may want to preplan discussion topics and questions before each stream; you can pull from them in case there's a lull in the chat. As you stream and gain experience, you'll find out what works best for you and your viewers.

To make the most out of your interaction with Twitch chatters, we encourage you to be engaging and empathetic. Being able to talk with viewers is one aspect of livestreaming, but making a connection to viewers on the other end of your broadcast can make the experience all the more rewarding for everyone involved. Some of the best moments captured on Twitch are those in which we see a genuine and heartfelt interaction between a broadcaster and his or her community.

LIVESTREAMER INTERVIEW: LittleSiha (Twitch.tv/LittleSiha)

Q: What advice can you give to livestreamers regarding how they interact with their viewers? What aspects do you think are the most important?

A: I really feel like, above all else, keeping it happy and upbeat is really important. I've found that a lot of my viewers hang out in my stream because they had a tough day at work or are going through something deep, and they really just need some positivity in their lives.

That being said, I think being very honest with your community and telling them when you're in a bad or sad mood is also important. The cool thing I've found with my community is that we work together; whenever someone in the chat room says they're sad, we all work together to make them feel better. When I'm feeling down, they do the same for me.

Q: Do you have advice for how to balance your focus on the game you're playing vs. your attention on viewers in chat?

A: I've noticed that I struggle with balancing my focus most when I'm playing a single-player game. Lots of cut scenes mean I'm staying focused on the game and end up ignoring the chat. The best thing you can do is keep an eye on the chat activity. If you notice the chat dying down a bit, focus less on a main story and more on something that takes less of your focus, like getting collectibles in an open-world game or buying new skins in a multiplayer game.

LIVESTREAMER INTERVIEW: The Hunter Wild (Twitch.tv/TheHunterWild)

Q: Do you have advice on interacting with viewers, and then analyzing those interactions later?

A: Remember that we're all human, and livestreaming is a uniquely human situation. You're a person, you're flawed, and you're going to mess up in the conversations sometimes. But as a streamer, you're also very interested in that stuff, and things will stick with you after the stream, good or bad.

A strange thing, being a streamer, is that you don't get to leave those things in the chat. It's work that's never just work; you don't get to leave it at the office. Streamers are inherently social and personal creatures, and engaging in any deep, meaningful, positive or negative discussion should stick with you. How you engage with the viewers in your chat should stick with you. When it does, I think it's also evidence that you're doing it right. When that's a lingering concern, I think it shows how important your connection to people is. You don't really consider that when you're having a good time in-stream, but in and after the negative moments, if you continue to think about your interactions, then that's evidence that you care deeply about your community.

Q: What stays with you? What are some things to watch out for?

A: I think some of this can depend on your brand, but by and large everyone will be roughly the same. People generally want the same things and interactions. Always keeping in mind that you have no idea what's going on in someone's life is one of the most important pieces to this.

Someone can be happy and joyous one day and be a complete jerk the next day. You shouldn't necessarily treat that one instance as the be-all and end-all of their being. You are a singular force, and no one else can be who you are in that moment during the livestream. When you're the center of attention, there's a serious responsibility there, which means you sometimes have to take lumps that you otherwise wouldn't take. If someone throws shade at you on a stream, you should keep in mind that it's entirely possible the person is going through some traumatic and tragic stuff. We don't know, because they're not our best friends and they're not sharing everything with us. Sometimes, they'll come in to your channel to just relax, or sometimes they feel comfortable enough to actually be in a bad mood around your channel, which is honestly kind of rare. To open up and be the person you don't want to be in front of other people, in a community that you are connected with, that really shows how deep a connection can be. That being said, it's really important for you, the streamer, to take the high road and be the bigger person so that hopefully the viewer comes out on the other side the next day feeling like you did them a service, like this is the community they belong in. And even if they never come back, it's something that can stick with them. You never know, and we all only have one life to live.

It's especially difficult if this is the tenth person to lash out at you that day, and you're emotionally heightened because you're human too. But you've got to do what you can to keep a cool head and treat everyone with a base level of dignity and respect. And you have to make sure you're in a good place, too. You are taking responsibility for other people as a broadcaster. It's something that's often overlooked, how heavy that responsibility can be. You're no one's therapist, and you shouldn't be treated as such, but you're trying to be everyone's friend. And that's a big thing.

Q: Do you actively set limits? Or have your limits evolved over time, in terms of how much you interact with viewers both on and off stream?

A: I have a very soft limit. I initially started with closed direct messages on social media, and it quickly became apparent that anyone who was watching a livestream could easily view the connection as a one-to-one relationship. Each one of the viewers sees one-to-one between him- or herself and the broadcaster. So, contacting the broadcaster directly seems very straightforward and obvious to them. It becomes very overwhelming for the broadcaster, and there can be a lot of guilt there. I know there was for me. I literally could not spend the time to talk to everyone on a one-to-one basis.

I had to put a hard line on the communications, and I had to create separate social media accounts for my moderators to use to manage the messages. And now, it's evolved to a point where we use both, and I have open direct messages. And I'm still trying to govern my time and personal communications with community members and viewers.

LIVESTREAMER INTERVIEW: missharvey (Twitch.tv/missharvey)

Q: What advice can you give to livestreamers regarding how they interact with viewers? What do you think is most important?

A: I think this is different for every streamer. You have some people who interact with their viewers a lot, you have others who take on really crazy characters, and there are others who don't say anything while they stream. Build your community and be yourself and see who sticks around.

For some, they enjoy watching quiet streamers because they don't like all the adrenaline and hyperactivity. I enjoy watching high-intensity streamers. I can't just watch a stream in the background; I need to be in it. It's why I watch livestreamers. So, just build your community and they will know how you are and what to expect. The consistent thing between all of this is respect for one another.

Lead the Conversation

No matter how you slice it, you are the center of attention for your livestream channel. It's your broadcast, your content, and your show! That means you often find yourself leading the discussion with Twitch chat during your streams. To continually create interesting and engaging discussions, you need to find out what works best for you, and how you can manage leading conversations while running your livestream. Some streamers can keep a conversation going for hours and hours, while others may need to fall back on specific talking points to reengage chatters. With so many frequent game announcements and conventions, you can almost always pull from current events to elicit discussions. What games are your viewers looking forward to and why? What events will they be traveling to in the near future?

A safe bet is to come up with a few generic questions to keep on hand to ask your viewers. These can be related to your stream or completely unrelated to the content you're displaying on your channel. Simple, open-ended questions, like, "What superpower would you have, if any?" or, "If you could travel back in time, when and where would you go?" can be easy for viewers to answer and can lead to interesting follow-up questions that stimulate further discussion in chat. You can also ask viewers to vote on things, such as what game you should stream next. Asking viewers what they thought about a particular scene or gameplay moment during your stream can elicit great chat reactions. You can also run new ideas past your viewers. What do they think of your new schedule? What kind of game should you play on the next stream? Your viewers can be a great source of inspiration and learning, so don't exclude them!

Be Proactive... and Reactive

In most cases, it's better to be proactive instead of reactive. But, in the case of livestreaming, both can be beneficial! Planning ahead for a livestream can be help you stay on course during a session. As you may already know, dividing your attention between production, content, and chat can be difficult. Having a basic run-of-show document or list of topics you want to discuss and games you want to play can keep you on course without having to rely on your memory for items you wanted to cover during the stream. Preparing a standard set of topics you discuss or share with viewers every livestream can get you in the habit of establishing the session—things like asking viewers how their days were, what they thought about recent events, and what they think about the game you're currently playing. Issuing a call to action, like reminding viewers to share a link to your channel on their social media sites, can create a steady rhythm and set expectations with regular viewers.

Being reactionary during a livestream, on the other hand, can lead to great stories and livestream clips. Did something unexpected happen during the campaign you're playing? Let your surprise show on stream! Did an incredible gameplay moment happen that you weren't expecting, making the difference between winning and losing the match? Show your excitement on stream and encourage your viewers to celebrate with you in chat with emotes and messages! These reaction moments don't have to happen all the time or in every livestream, but when they do, it never hurts to express your reaction outwardly and share a genuine moment with your viewers.

 TIP: Reaction moments can be "clippable." They are good 5- to 30-second scenes that you or your viewers can clip from a broadcast and share with unique links. You can then add a custom command to re-share this link from time to time, to remind viewers of the good times shared on your channel.

Know Your Limits

In an age where many of the most popular Twitch streamers are larger-than-life personalities, it can be difficult to determine where you fit in with all the others. The pressure to perform and live up to preconceived expectations is daunting and sometimes overwhelming, but realizing that you must first be true to yourself and then build on your established platform can be a great key to success.

First, take some time to reflect on your personality and determine what types of interactions work best for you. Are you an extroverted person who gains energy and excitement by being around people, or are you more introverted and require downtime to recover energy? Are you naturally good at striking up conversations and getting people to share their views and opinions, or do you like to answer questions more than ask them, and wait to see where the discussion leads? Understanding these things can help you establish a rhythm for streaming (stream duration, pre-planning discussion topics, etc.) and better prepare you for when you go live. Don't adopt an online persona that you can't continuously support unless you have a stream rhythm that works well for you, and especially avoid creating an online role if that style doesn't suit your personality.

Next, control your expectations for what streaming life is like. Understand that you may not be able to stream as often as you want, for as long as you want. You may be inclined to dive right in and give it your all, which is great! But in reality, this is an easy way to burn out quickly. This especially occurs if you put a lot of time into something and get little out of it, which will happen if you don't control your expectations and start small.

Some streamers can stream every morning, afternoon, or evening for hours on end, while others can only stream once a week for a couple of hours in one session. Set a stream schedule that works well for your personal life. Do you have a daytime job and can only stream on weeknights? Do you have a family that needs your support throughout the week, so you have only a few hours to stream on weekends?

Are you exploring livestreaming as a potential full-time job, so your days are free to stream whenever you want? All of these schedules are manageable and can lead to success if you go in with an open mind and realistic expectations. Starting small and setting a solid schedule can help your consistency and overall stream performance. Setting a schedule to stream twice a week, for two hours each session, and keeping that schedule consistent for two to three months can have a great impact on establishing a viewership community that will support you.

Finally, determine what you will and won't tolerate in chat. This includes your interactions with viewers, but also between viewers within your chat. If you have mods, be sure to meet with them periodically to discuss what interactions warrant a timeout or a ban in chat. Take some time to define boundaries for when playful language and teasing turns into bullying and aggression. Establish chat rules and display them on your channel, or create a custom command that displays the chat rules periodically via a third-party program. For example, if you don't want to tolerate game spoilers in chat, establish that as a rule and clearly state the consequences for breaking it. The more transparent and consistent you are with your channel rules, the better it will be for everyone involved. It can be awkward and sometimes difficult to timeout or ban people in chat, and online communication often falls into grey areas, so taking time to contemplate what you will and won't tolerate can make it easier to approach these situations as they occur while you're livestreaming.

LIVESTREAMER INTERVIEW: wgrates (Twitch.tv/wgrates)

Q: What advice can you give on setting a stream schedule?

A: Start small when you first start broadcasting, even if you aren't working full-time. Don't burn yourself out.

When I started, my inclination was to jump right in and stream seven days a week and grow the channel like crazy, and I had to remind myself that this was going to burn me out. So, I did that for a little while to find out what my best streaming hours were, and as soon as I found those, then I backed off on the schedule. I made sure to take time to myself, take a day off from streaming, have time to unwind. Streaming takes a lot out of you. You need to schedule your time off. Wednesdays are my days off, and I make sure I don't touch a computer at all on those days.

Be gentle on yourself. You may want to start streaming and then realize that streaming just isn't for you. And there's nothing wrong with that. It's important to remember that. If it's not for you, then great—you didn't lose a lot of money or time or investment in that case, because you started small. And if it is for you, then you can slowly upgrade. You can make small changes and upgrades, and you can be successful like this.

LIVESTREAMER INTERVIEW: missharvey (Twitch.tv/missharvey)

Q: What advice can you give on balancing your attention between gameplay and the chat?

A: This is the most difficult part. The more involved I am in my chat, the less well I play the game. Some people will pop in and ask if I even reply to chat, because so many pro gamers who stream focus solely on the game. The key is balance, and if I'm not interacting with my teammates in game, then I should be interacting with people in chat. Sometimes I get really into the game and I forget about the stream for a couple minutes. I'd rather focus on the game, and when there's a clear moment to switch then I'll interact with chat. I can't do both things at once, and this is how I can be satisfied with my energy level on stream.

Q: Do you actively set limits? Or have your limits evolved over time in terms of how much you interact with viewers both on and off stream?

A: While I'm streaming, I talk to viewers as much as I can. When I'm not streaming, I interact on a third-party chat service and on social media. I don't do direct messages. So, if people want to talk to me, they have to do it in public channels. That really helps and keeps people honest. It's a better distinction between casual conversations and friendship-level conversations, too.

I try to talk in my social channels every day, but if I get really busy then I'll just answer questions if there are any. I have a community manager who will post content and keep conversations going. I think the best system for this is through a third-party chat server; it's the best way to feel included in a community and feels more permanent than social media posts that can be missed if you don't check them often enough.

Interacting with Streamers

Interacting and working with other streamers can be an excellent way to reach new audiences and provide unique content for your viewers. But how do you make those connections? How do you catch the eyes of your favorite streamers with the hope they will work with you on some livestream events or casual co-streams?

TIP: Livestreamers are people too, with their own schedules, goals, and personalities. Finding other like-minded livestreamers can be easier than you think, but it's all a matter of how you approach it.

Establishing connections with other streamers starts with supporting them. A great first step is to get involved in their livestreams and communities. Join in the discussions in their chat, get to know them and their regular viewers, and show them your personality as well. If you have the chance to attend conventions and meet streamers in person, having a face-to-face connection is a great option. It never hurts to network with other livestreamers, and you can always join their communities to ask them for their opinions and best practices. We'll talk more about networking in the Networking chapter.

LIVESTREAMER INTERVIEW: wgrates (Twitch.tv/wgrates)

Q: What advice can you give to livestreamers regarding how they interact with viewers and other streamers? What do you think is most important?

A: Be very respectful of other streamers' communities. If you're in another channel's chat, and they don't know you're a streamer, then don't just bring it up unless they prompt you to. I go into other streamers' channels all the time, and I'll just talk with them and their viewers, and I never once bring up my channel.

Treat them like how you'd want to see a chatter in your community act. Some people don't care if chatters come in and talk about their streams, but it's better to assume that not everyone is like you. All streamers work hard for their channels and their communities, so don't throw respect out the window just because you might be okay with people promoting their streams in your channel.

Every channel, every community has rules. Be respectful of those.

LIVESTREAMER INTERVIEW: LittleSiha (Twitch.tv/LittleSiha)

Q: What advice can you give to livestreamers regarding how they interact with other livestreamers? What do you think is most important to keep in mind regarding this?

A: This answer is going to sound so cliche, but it's totally true—keep it natural! I enjoy the company of other streamers most when we're not talking about streaming, but what games or developers we love. Your intentions will also be pretty obvious; if you're talking to a streamer because you think you can gain something from being friends with them, it will be an immediate turnoff. I personally have a lot of fun going into streams I've never been in before and hanging out with their community or talking about the game they're playing. Keep it very relaxed.

Hosting

When you're offline, you can host other livestream content on your channel. Hosting other streamers is an excellent way to show support and it encourages those streamers to host your content on their channel in the future. You can host a channel by typing **/host <name>** into your chat window, and if the other streamer has alerts set up on their channel, then you may see a Host notification pop up on their stream.

In Twitch settings, you can also select streamers to auto-host on your channel when you're offline. This way, your channel will always show their content, even if you're not around to host them manually. A very successful hosting tactic is to host directly after you conclude your livestream, so that all the current viewers you have will see the hosted streamer's content as well. Depending on how many viewers you have at the time, you could end up giving the streamer a big boost in views! In general, this is a good practice, and other streamers will remember and thank you for it, usually by giving you a shout out on their streams or hosting your content on their channels as well.

Raiding

Similar to hosting, you can also "raid" another streamer's channel during their livestream. A raid is when you encourage your livestream viewers to go to a different Twitch channel and engage with their community through posting messages in their chat, following their channel, and subscribing. Almost simultaneously, you will then end your livestream and immediately host the other channel's content.

Raids are generally good-natured and can be exciting events for streamers and viewers. However, some streamers do not approve of them. Raids can be disruptive and break the flow of the other streamers' content, or raids can be missed entirely if they happen during a multiplayer or fast-paced game, when the streamer isn't paying attention to the chat. If possible, you should gauge how the other streamer will react to a raid and see what the streamer is doing on their livestream before you raid them.

Twitch officially supports raiding streamers via the **/raid <name>** command in chat. This allows the streamer to start a countdown of 30 seconds to the raid and it joins all your current viewers in the raid by default. Viewers can opt to leave the raid by clicking the Leave button at the top of the chat window. At the end of the countdown, the Twitch Raid feature automatically begins hosting the new channel and displays a message in the other streamer's channel with the text, "<Your channel> is raiding with a party of <number of raiders>." You don't need to use the official Twitch Raid feature to raid another channel, but it's helpful to use the feature if you're new to raiding, or if you want your channel information to be captured in the Recent Raids field on the streamer's dashboard.

Twitch provides some safeguards for streamers who want to limit or disable the official Raid feature on their channels. In the dashboard settings, streamers can limit raids to only a select few streamers, or they can shut down raiding altogether. In the event of a manual raid (one not conducted through the Raid feature), a streamer can stop the raid by changing the chat to follower or subscriber-only for a short time. This limits or stops the number of spammed raid messages posted by the raiding viewers.

LIVESTREAMER INTERVIEW: The Hunter Wild (Twitch.tv/TheHunterWild)

Q: What advice can you give to livestreamers regarding how they interact with viewers? What do you think is most important?

A: Specifically, when I raid a channel, I stick around and speak to the streamer and their community. It's that bridge, much like if you bring two groups of people together in real life, you don't just shove your group at the other group and go, "Hey guys, go talk about, I dunno, cats. Bye!" You are the bridge, and at all points you need to remember how humans communicate. People often feel uncomfortable in new situations and new places, and presumably the viewers that come over in your raid care for and respect you, so you need to do some work to bring the groups together, not just hope they enjoy it.

Part of that etiquette, on the side of the viewers that are already there in the channel you're raiding, is to have some sort of responsibility for their community, too. Everyone should still conduct themselves properly and respectfully. Help to keep the new people really comfortable, and the raiding broadcaster should be in there, getting their viewers excited about the new streamer they're watching. It's sort of like being a politician, police officer, and best friend all at the same time.

Overall, streamer etiquette is simultaneously a very wide and deep river. A lot of points across there can be very challenging to navigate, stuff that I'm still thinking and working my way through.

Co-Streaming

Once you get to know a few streamers, you can approach them to co-stream with you. A co-stream is where two (or more) streamers stream at the same time on their respective channels, but they play games with the other streamers. These streamers are sometimes in the same game lobby or voice chat server together, so you can hear all the audio feeds from each streamer. You could also have a more interactive co-stream event involving shared video feeds, discussion topics, and shared game commentary. For example, have one streamer play the game while both streamers talk in real-time and react to the game and chat, or do a talk-show-style livestream.

Co-streaming can be a fantastic way to bridge viewership across the channels and create unique content. Some of the most successful co-streamed events can involve two or more streamers commenting on the same gameplay or focusing on a shared goal. For example, streams geared toward fund raising donations for charity and that involve many streamers can be very successful and they help promote the streamers involved in the event.

Join a Team

Livestreaming teams are composed of two or more livestreamers for the purpose of promoting team members' channels and finding business opportunities to support future stream events and new livestreamers. Some teams are self-managed and funded, while others are run by a group of people who manage the team's financial, legal, and branding concerns. Teams can be formed around any idea, genre, or theme. Twitch currently supports livestream teams in a limited capacity; teams can create Twitch Team pages that display each team member's video feed, and livestreamers can fill out a Team field on their Stream Information page in the dashboard.

 TIP: You can start your own livestream team or join a pre-existing one— the criteria for joining teams are different across the board. You can also start a livestream team outside the official Twitch Team capacity. However, the option to display the team name in the Team field on Twitch will not be an option if you take this path.

Currently, only partnered Twitch streamers can create an official Twitch Team, meaning the team is recognized on the Twitch platform and can be displayed on a channel's page below the video feed. If you are invited to join a team, you will find the invite listed under My Teams in the Settings - Channel and Videos section of Twitch. You can accept or deny invites, and remove your team affiliations at any time via the Settings tab.

Teams can be an excellent way to network and support other streamers while getting more exposure for your channel, but you should be aware of the strengths, weaknesses, and pitfalls associated with any team affiliation.

You can join as many teams as you want on Twitch, however the benefit of joining teams ebbs and flows depending on the situation and timeliness of your participation. Understand that joining a team doesn't usually mean a free ride to affiliate, partnership, or Twitch glory—it means you're now invested in the success of the team, and you therefore need to add your time, effort, and support in order to get benefit out of the team partnership. Generally, the team will require some level of daily, weekly, or monthly participation. This can equate to dedicating some of your streaming time to the team channel, or some degree of content creation and hosting/promoting the team's content on your own channel and social media sites.

If you join multiple teams, you should be aware of their target audiences and branding themes or dedicated genres. If you join five teams that all share the target audience of a particular first-person shooter game, then you'll likely reach the same audience members you would have if you had joined just one or two of those teams. Some degree of cannibalization for your audience is okay if you join multiple teams, but diversifying your membership across teams that promote content to different types of audiences can expand your growth potential.

If you start or join a Twitch Team (one that is verified on the Twitch platform), then you can access the Twitch Team page. The Team page is a hub for all the streamers of a given team. You can see all the team members listed in one area, a live feed player in the middle of the page, and details about the team below. It's a hybrid of a standard Twitch channel, but includes links and references to the team members and doesn't include a chat window. Teams often have a Twitch account as well, which functions like any other streamer account—this allows team members to stream directly to and auto-host from the team account.

If you're just starting to livestream, or you have some experience but want to learn more, then joining a team could help set you off on the right foot. You can learn a lot about promoting and branding from a team, as well as how to network and navigate business opportunities.

Ultimately, a team consists of multiple streamers all working toward shared goals. Communication is key, especially if the team depends on you for something, or you need support from team management or other team members. Remember that everyone has strengths and weaknesses, so working with a team of like-minded individuals that support one another and share a common cause can be exciting and rewarding.

LIVESTREAMER INTERVIEW: TheMavShow (Twitch.tv/TheMavShow)

Q: Has your perception of stream teams changed over time?

A: Yes! I have been on a few stream teams and have learned so much. I've had great triumphs and failures, and it's all part of finding your place and meeting new people. It's crucial to work well with others, to be open and honest about feelings, and to care about the work you're doing. Much like networking and getting to know other casters, you have to care. Period. A team is a great collaboration and can even be considered a family. My current stream team is incredible, and I can't rave enough about my streaming family.

LIVESTREAMER INTERVIEW: missharvey (Twitch.tv/missharvey)

Q: What was it about joining or starting a gaming team that got you interested in pursuing it?

A: It's great being part of a community. In being part of an organization on Twitch, you can see other streamers and support each other. Sometimes, the tools and features provided to livestream teams can be more beneficial for the team owners rather than the individual streamers. The teams want streamers on their teams to increase their stats and reach, so it's very important to them. I think for smaller streamers, joining a team can be very beneficial. If you're already an established streamer, then joining a team may not be very helpful for you.

Q: How has the competitive gaming team, or your experience on a team, shaped your livestreaming plans and goals?

A: It's awful! When I'm really training with my competitive team, I can't stream at all. Some practice games we could stream, and some teams stream their practices overall, but in general we don't. We keep everything hidden. So, if I want to stream as well, then I need to invest two to three more hours of game time on top of my eight to nine hours of practice that day.

That means I'm going to game for 10, 11, or 12 hours a day. Streaming and competitive gaming is awful. My livestream community is into my competitive game, so if I'm going to stream, it's going to be the same game that I'm practicing already. There's no break.

Q: What advice would you give to other livestreamers who are looking to join or start a team, be it competitive or casual livestreaming?

A: Schedule! Even if you're only streaming an hour a day, if you always do it at the same time, then people will show up. When my schedule was busy and I was practicing all the time, I would stream for one hour and call it my "warm up" stream, and people would show up! I'd call it my super fast stream, and I would do everything fast. Super fast raffles where you have one minute to join. Everything was themed for being fast, and it worked out well. But I was also consistent and I would show up every day at the same time. That's the most difficult part as a streamer; it means you have to push yourself to be there on time and go live at a specific time every day. It's very challenging.

Third-Party Tools and Features

Broadcasting Applications

Console and PC livestreamers differ in their stream setups. The ability to stream directly from a console can be convenient, as the broadcaster uses the stream features built directly into the console. This means things are pre-configured in a standard way for all users of that particular platform. This makes it a good option to try if you want to start streaming but you're not sure where to begin or even if streaming is really for you. The setup process and customization changes drastically for broadcasters who stream from their computers. PC streamers use third-party broadcasting applications to capture their gameplay, webcam, and audio feeds, sending that data to display on their Twitch channels.

Broadcasting applications allow numerous customizations. They usually allow for multiple "scenes" to which a broadcaster can transition at any time during his or her livestream. These scenes can be individually set up to display different gameplay and webcam variations. For example, some streamers create a "Starting Soon" scene, which usually displays the message with a countdown timer. They display this scene at the beginning, when they first start their livestream, to allow time for viewers to enter the channel and get ready for the real show to begin.

 TIP: At its core, a broadcasting application allows a streamer to create multiple scenes by pulling in different sources. A source can range from a media file, to a screen capture, to a device like a webcam. Semi-professional and professional streamers use broadcasting applications to design scenes that showcase their technical setup and channel branding.

For more advanced streamers, or streamers looking to really customize their livestreams per event, day, or game, broadcasting applications can provide the ability to save an entire presentation. This means all the scenes and their associated files and source links are saved, and you can load different presentations depending on what sort of setup you want for your upcoming stream.

You can choose from a number of different broadcasting applications, and they range in price. Depending on the type of content you want to create on Twitch, you may not need a very robust program for creating and transitioning between scenes. Twitch recommends some applications under the Streaming Tools section of the dashboard.

LIVESTREAMER INTERVIEW: missharvey (Twitch.tv/missharvey)

Q: What features do you look for when you try broadcasting software or tools? What's most important to you?

A: Because I use so many computers and I stream from so many devices, and even from different cities, countries, and events, the feature I look for most is being able to log in and all of my settings are saved. Something where I don't have to redo it every time. In the past, this was a big pain. Recently, some programs have updated so when you log in, it saves everything. You can create scenes and save it throughout, no matter where you are, as soon as you download the application and log in again, it all works. That was the biggest win for my stream because now I don't have to have complicated livestream setups when I go to conferences and events.

Overlays and Notifications

Another category of tools are those that focus on the art assets and overlays that display on a livestreamer's channel. Have you ever seen a notification display onscreen when someone subscribed to a livestreamer's channel? Most likely, that streamer used an external broadcasting tool that provided stream alerts and notifications.

Livestreamers use notification and overlay tools to customize the types of notifications that display on their channel during a stream. Most broadcasters show notifications for common and noteworthy actions, such as new follows, subscriptions, donations, and charity initiatives. Many programs allow a livestreamer to customize the duration, sound effects, position, and look of a notification: art assets, static images, gifs, and so forth. Some programs even allow for randomization of these notifications, so you can ensure the same exact wording doesn't display twice or three times in a row on your channel.

Notifications and alerts can be some of the most fun and engaging parts of a livestream. Setting these up can take time, and you'll need to run a variety of tests to ensure all your connections are up and running. The more personality and branding you can put into your alerts and notifications, the more viewers will want to participate in your channel and trigger them onscreen.

LIVESTREAMER INTERVIEW: missharvey (Twitch.tv/missharvey)

Q: What kind of overlays do you use on your stream? Which notifications and alerts are most important, and why?

A: Notifications are super important, as that's what can motivate people to subscribe, donate, and follow. When my webcam is full screen, I put the chat onscreen as well. I think some people like to read it, and it creates some sort of second-level interaction with me. I also have sponsors, so I rotate in their logos and messaging as well. In terms of layout, I keep my sponsors pretty small onscreen. I keep them to maybe five percent of the screen real estate. Then I scale chat up to about 20 percent of the screen when I'm full screen and not showing gameplay.

Bots

Bots are externally developed programs or applications that have admin (or moderator) level access to your livestream channel. They're designed to enhance the stream experience for viewers, be helpful and relevant to the broadcaster, and can be fully customized to fit your channel's brand and experience goals. Many different types of bots are available, and small-, medium-, and large-scale streamers use bots in a variety of different ways. Before you select a bot, research the different types available and determine what feature sets you want to use. It's also imperative to use stable and trustworthy bots that don't pose a security risk to your channel or your personal information.

Due to the customizable nature of bots, there tend to be many tools and features; learn about and modify a bot's tools before fully incorporating it into your channel. Researching, customizing, and testing a bot can take time, and you'll want to know exactly how your bot operates before you go live with it. Livestreaming can be a pressured experience, and the last thing you want to do is add the stress of troubleshooting a bot while on a live show. Bots also regularly get updates and new features, so setting aside some time on a regular basis to read about and test new features can keep you up to date.

Bots: Custom Commands

You can tell that a bot is running on a channel if you see a mod account with "bot" in the name, or you see a mod account posting very standard and immediate replies to viewers in chat. One common example is to have a bot say, "welcome to the channel" to new viewers or, "thank you" to viewers that follow your channel.

EXAMPLE: If a new viewer follows your channel while you're live on Twitch, a bot can recognize this follow action and display a pre-written message in the chat box, such as, "Thank you <name> for following my channel! Welcome to the team!"

As we mentioned in a previous section of this book, Twitch standard commands start with "**/**" (without the quotation marks). External commands via a bot are slightly different, in that they start with "**!**" (again, without the quotation marks). Many bots allow streamers to create their own commands, which can be straightforward or complex in nature. If you want to share information about your channel via a bot, then you can create commands for anyone in chat to use. They can range from information about your history on Twitch, to your gaming PC or console specs, to your livestream schedule. Or, you can create timed commands that run on a preset timer while your channel is live.

EXAMPLE: Every 30 minutes, the bot will post the command !schedule, which will then trigger the streamer's schedule information to post in the chat box, such as "Streams happen every Monday, Wednesday, and Friday from 1-3 p.m. Pacific."

Bots: Features and Uses

There are a lot of things to keep in mind while you livestream, and providing pertinent information to your viewers in a timely manner can be a challenge. Timed messages can help! You can use them to show important information to new viewers, and they can also remind new and regular viewers to do a "call to action." A good example of this is to set a timed message that reminds viewers to share the stream on social media (the call to action). The more people who share your channel, the more likely you'll get new viewers. Even if you don't remember to verbally ask your viewers to share the stream while you're live, your bot won't forget!

Some popular custom commands are for social media links and caster shout-outs. For example, the **!social** command can trigger the bot to post your links to any number of social platforms. The command **!caster <name>** can trigger a message that points viewers to another streamer's channel, including a message like "Check out **<name>** channel and give them a follow!"

Some bots offer extensive features to keep your viewers engaged in Twitch chat. The type of bot you select for your channel will depend heavily on what sort of experience you want to give your viewers and what features are supported by the bot.

If most of your streams feature multiplayer games and you want to give viewers an opportunity to play with you, consider finding a bot that has a "queue" feature. When enabled in the bot, this allows viewers to type a command in chat (usually **!join**) to add their name to the queue list. The bot can then pick names from the list in order or at random, and you and your mods can then reach out to those individual viewers for their gamertags to find them in-game. Some bots even allow you to limit who can join the queue based on specific criteria, such as followers or subs only.

Some bots allow you to track and manage entries for giveaways that you host on your stream. Similar to the queue feature, bots can allow viewers to type a command in chat (sometimes called **!raffle** or **!joingiveaway**) to join the pool of entries. You can limit the participants by criteria or allow anyone to join. Some giveaway features will send a message to chat detailing what you can win (the streamer enters this information into the bot), and can even show timers for the giveaway deadline. You can use the bot to pick a winner, and their name will display in the Twitch chat for all to see. As the streamer hosting the giveaway, it will be your responsibility to provide the prize to the winner upon selecting a name from the pool of entries. Twitch also requires some standard wording to use on prize giveaways, so it's best to consult the Twitch Terms of Service before you begin.

Streamers can utilize bots with a currency or points feature, which allows viewers to earn points based on the duration of time they watch the Twitch channel. Some streamers provide points only when their channel is live, and some allow points to be accumulated while the stream is offline as well. Points can be used for a number of different things, most notably as criteria for joining in with other features, such as the queue or giveaway features we discussed earlier. Thresholds can be added to point systems, so users who accumulate a lot of points can work toward higher-ranked tiers in the system. Generally, these ranks don't impact things too drastically, and are more like "badges of honor" for which viewers strive. Ranks can be an easy way to see which viewers have been around the longest, and they can be a fun way to reward viewers and incentivize them to reach higher-ranked tiers. As with most bot features, the points feature (and all systems therein) can be tailored to your particular stream experience.

Some of the most advanced bots on Twitch have integrated currency systems with in-chat games. These games are based on viewers bidding or leveraging a certain amount of points for the chance to win more points. One popular currency-based Twitch chat game found in many bots is called Heist, which allows viewers to opt-in via chat and place bets on how well the fictional bank heist will go. The bot walks viewers through the game scenario and calculates the outcome on its own, winning or losing points, by team or per individual, based on a weighted algorithm or random number generation. This is just one example of the various points- and currency-based games available through chat bots. Depending on the type of stream experience you want to provide, you can enable points-based games in chat and encourage viewers to get involved, or just let viewers run the games whenever they want.

Voice Chat Services

Similar to bots, voice chat services are externally created programs that can enhance the livestream experience for the streamer and the viewers. A voice chat service provides a platform where multiple people can speak to one another through text or voice communication. Often, these services provide connections through servers that can be customized by the server owner. Customizations include making text and voice channels, creating user roles to limit functionality for user types, and making access to different channels available to the various user roles.

In standard and advanced practice, streamers tend to prefer programs that allow for stability and flexibility while livestreaming. As you continue to evolve your livestream channel and content creation, you'll find that controlling the audio outputs of your programs can be important and sometimes difficult to manage. The more direct control you have over volume adjustment by channel or by person, as well as notification sounds and alerts via the voice chat program, the better off you'll be. Imagine a scenario where a streamer wants to livestream a multiplayer game with two other people. In some cases, the streamer will speak with his or her partners via the in-game chat system (if it exists within the game they're playing). Some games provide the ability to adjust overall voice volumes (globally), but more often than not this control is limited. Now, let's say one partner has a bad microphone, which makes him or her very hard to hear. Using an external voice chat system outside the game platform can provide more control over volume per person, allowing the streamer to boost the volume of the partner with the bad mic, while keeping others at a standard volume level. A program that provides audio flexibility and customization, and standardizes that level of access regardless of game or content, can be critical.

Many voice chat services come with text channels, or the ability for written communication between users. Some services provide more in-depth functionality, like link sharing or embedded images and videos. Some livestreamers have found when fostering a community for their Twitch channel, it can be beneficial to provide viewers with an external place to speak with each other when the stream is offline. Voice chat services can help by providing this shared, independent space. Depending on the program's features, a streamer can set user roles to provide different levels of access. The main channels (voice and/or text) can be public to all users, while some channels can be used for your admins and mods for planning and management discussions. Channels can be created around different purposes and discussion topics, like spoilers for new games and movies, or updates on gaming news. Considering the voice chat service as a hub for information around the streamer and his or her schedule, but also providing a place for viewers to get to know each other outside of the Twitch livestream, can provide a positive and lasting community experience.

When you look into a third-party voice chat service, think about the common issues that arise when you stream games (or other content) that involve multiple people speaking. In reviewing the services, determine whether the features will help you create better content by giving you greater control of the situation. Can you adjust volume by person? Can the service provide text channels, images, and links? Can you adjust settings and channel access by user type or role?

As with all added features, setting up and maintaining a voice chat service for your livestream viewers can take some effort. Understanding the system you want to implement will take time and testing. Getting some hands-on experience can be the best way to learn, so consider joining another livestreamer's voice chat program to see how others use these features to their benefit.

LIVESTREAMER INTERVIEW: SirSlaw (Twitch.tv/SirSlaw)

Q: What are some of your favorite commands?

A: I created my own Twitch chat bot. I've been building tools for livestreamers for a couple of years now, and this particular one is a tool that I envisioned years ago, when I first discovered Twitch. I found that at a certain point, some channels would transition from community and engagement-focused channels to entertainment-focused. There's nothing wrong with this, but one of the big selling points of Twitch and this medium is that it's interactive at heart. Some of these larger channels tend to lose that community connection. So, I took this idea and decided to build a tool that would increase engagement. It would affect the relationships between viewers, and between viewers and the livestreamers.

There were a lot of positive side effects from using a tool like this. I had no idea it would have this sort of impact on viewer engagement across the board for my channel. It's what allowed me to be full-time since day zero. My favorite part, or the part that has had the most impact for me, is the fact that a lot of people and other companies that approach the livestream space develop tools that put the livestreamer first. They're primarily focused on helping the broadcaster raise money, and that's not really what a lot of us are here for. It's certainly not why your viewers are here. So, my tool focuses on the viewers first, and their relationships with each other, and their individual relationships with the broadcaster.

Your Community and Being a Leader

As you continue to stream, gain experience, and grow your Twitch channel, you'll start to foster a community of regular viewers. How you interact with them is the first step in determining how to lead them. That's right, leadership! You may not have thought much about it until now, but many livestreamers who begin to build communities become the de facto leaders of these communities. It's your livestream, your community, and leadership goes hand-in-hand with creating something all your own.

The term leadership can be intimidating. What does it mean to lead others? What does it take to be a good leader? Can I designate others to be the leader (yes, maybe)? While leading others and setting examples is challenging, getting into the right mind-set can be a great first step to becoming a good leader and managing your community for success.

So, what does all this mean? At its core, leadership is acting and speaking in a way that motivates and manages others. You don't necessarily need to focus and think about leadership to set a good example. You can hone and adhere to the qualities of a good leader as you grow your channel and community, including being honest, inspiring others to achieve their goals, and being creative.

Steps to Leadership

First, leading a community requires you to know yourself and what you're willing to tolerate in your communication with others. Let's go back to the section on Knowing Your Limits to help build this foundation. As a broadcaster, you keep your content's pace consistent by sticking to a livestream schedule. Looking through the lens of community leadership, you're expected to set the schedule first and communicate with viewers before, during, and after your livestreams for any schedule changes and the reasons for those changes. As we mentioned previously, the schedule you set doesn't have to be intensive, but it should be consistent. For example, streaming once a week for two hours is enough to establish a pace for content, set expectations for viewers, and entice people to return to your channel at those scheduled times.

TIP: Set a schedule that works well for you, without burning yourself out or giving too much of yourself. Streaming too much and not recharging can limit your ability to create compelling content, and it may burn you out from livestreaming altogether.

Next, get your mods up to speed and on the same page regarding community leadership. As moderators, they are well-versed in the management side of running the channel and should reinforce your goals and views of the community. Take some time to reiterate the rules of the stream, what you will and won't tolerate in interactions between streamer, viewers, and moderators, and set communication standards with the team (e.g., all communications done through Twitch messages, or on a voice chat service, etc.). Set an example for your mods illustrating the kind of leadership you're striving for. Your leadership style will most likely spread through your moderators and into your community.

The biggest element in leading a community is your own interaction with viewers. Do you always take a few seconds to welcome new and returning viewers? Do you facilitate conversation and discussion amongst viewers? Do you provide content that caters to a particular viewership market or game genre? It takes time to refine the skills you need to produce live content and connect with viewers in chat. Remembering to set a good example and treating others how you want to be treated in every livestream helps make this a habit.

As you begin to focus on leadership, you may want to review previous broadcasts to analyze your interactions and identify areas you can improve. This is a great way to gain insight into how you perceive and deliver messages on your stream. You can also solicit feedback from trusted viewers and moderators to help guide your interactions. Good leaders should always want to improve themselves and those around them, and being open to feedback and constructive criticism benefits you in the long run. And of course, watching and learning from other streamers who produce the kind of content you want to create helps, too!

In all this experimenting and content creation, remember to take a step back and recall your goals: the kind of content you're trying to create, the kind of community you want to foster, and why you wanted to livestream in the first place. It's easy to get sidelined by small details or big agendas, but remember that this is your community and your content, and you ultimately get to call the shots. Adjustments and revisions are necessary with any undertaking like this, as no one executes it perfectly the first time. Take the feedback and perceptions you gain with a grain of salt. The more data you have to pull from, the better your chances of making the right decisions for you, your channel, and your peers.

LIVESTREAMER INTERVIEW: The Hunter Wild (Twitch.tv/TheHunterWild)

Q: When you first started livestreaming, did you think much about becoming a community leader or what that meant?

A: Absolutely, that goes hand-in-hand with why I started streaming in the first place. Being together with others is the main purpose of life, and I also feel there is and will continue to be a grand importance and responsibility for people to create communities that lift up and guide culture.

I feel we're at a critical and pivotal point in the way human beings as a whole communicate with each other and create culture. I considered it my responsibility to learn the best ways that other broadcasters and "good people in society's eyes" do this, and create a place where the best versions of culture can continue to thrive and be spread to people who may otherwise be missing them. It's easy to get caught up in the bad on the internet. I wanted to create a place and govern it in the best and most heartfelt way. That was my purpose, before I ever started streaming. It's a matter of how much you want to contribute, and where.

LIVESTREAMER INTERVIEW: Sir Slaw (Twitch.tv/SirSlaw)

Q: What do you think makes a good community leader, or influencer?

A: I think it's someone who has empathy. They don't just have IQ; they also have EQ. It's very important for a community leader to understand, and I mean have the capacity, ability, and decision making to choose to listen to people, and to do things as a result of listening to people in their community. I can't overemphasize the EQ thing. Emotional intelligence is something we don't put a lot of stock in, because it's very hard to quantify, but there's no more valuable trait than being capable of empathizing with people. And even if you can't respond in chat to everyone, they need to feel empathized with. People need to feel that, not just have it happen.

You, the Influencer

The term influencer is relatively new in a marketing and social media context. It's used throughout the gaming industry, and it refers to someone who's prominent, or someone who can influence the thoughts and decisions of others. In the broadest sense of the word, we are all influencers—we influence our friends, coworkers, and families daily. In livestreaming, the term influencer also refers to those who have followers on social media and content-creation sites like Twitch. These are two extremes, from passive influences in your daily life, to assertive influences in online mediums upon large audiences, and everyone falls somewhere within this spectrum.

You've likely seen a few content pieces created by big influencers who were hired by companies to market brands or products to their followers. Though some people strive to achieve this level of influence and success on Twitch, it's by no means the only success criteria, nor the only way for someone to be influential. As a Twitch streamer creating content for the public, you need to understand that you are an influencer. You may not have huge reach across thousands of viewers (yet), but getting any number of viewers means that people are tuning in to your content. That means they are listening to what you have to say.

To some, the term influencer might be viewed in a negative light. It's meant to differentiate some people from others, and in this case, the people separated are those with communities of followers. Livestreamers don't necessarily want to be separated by labels; they want to interact and engage with people. It's hard to make genuine connections with people if titles or classes define your position. The term may sometimes be viewed negatively from a social perspective, but on the flip side, companies and developers often prefer to work more with influencers than everyday streamers. This is where the differentiation can be a good thing if you can wield the term wisely.

By calling you an influencer, we don't intend to stress you out—it's a reminder that your words and actions can impact others. Be mindful of how you present yourself and your content to viewers. Try to consider how you would react to things as a Twitch viewer, and adjust your actions accordingly. Some viewers post mean or disrespectful comments in chat to see if they get a rise out of you—don't take the bait. Some viewers ask for your opinion on current events or personal matters, and it's up to you to decide how you answer those questions, if at all. There's a fine line between being true to yourself and being a leader for your community, and the two concepts don't necessarily have to be at odds. However, you sometimes need to make a decision to react in a way that better fits with being a leader or a good influencer.

Q: Some people have a problem with the word influencer being used to describe who they are. Do you have any thoughts about why this might be?

A: I think part of it is humility, where you want to appear as though you're humble. You may very well be. I want to appear as though I'm humble, and I like to think that I am, but within that very statement there's a touch of arrogance. But there's a difference between a surface humility and heartfelt humility. True humility is the ability to be shown where you can improve, where you're wrong, where your faults lie, with an open heart so you can change to be better.

To some extent, we want to imply that we're not a big deal, when we really are. I don't think it's arrogant to accept that you actually play a role in what other people think by virtue of your position. It's just a reality. You can treat it a number of ways, but that's simply going to be a fact. You are influencing perspectives and hearts and minds, and taking that seriously is vital. If you don't, you run the risk of doing or saying something that causes harm. If you accept that you are an influencer, then you'll give more weight and import to the things you say and do.

Q: What do you think of being considered an influencer? Is there anything important about this idea that you'd like to express to other livestreamers?

A: Being an influencer never really dawned on me throughout the years. The only time I realized I was called an influencer was a couple years ago. When I was contacting game developers to test their games, I would say that I was a streamer. They'd always say no to working with me. Then, one day someone said I should change the word streamer to influencer. The next time I contacted companies, I said I was an influencer and I provided some analytics, and the reception was very positive.

For me, the word influencer is more of an analytical term. Now that I have a bigger grasp of the meaning of influencer, I think it's our job to shape our communities. I've molded through influencing my community in certain ways. For example, if we get a viewer in chat that gives me a backhanded compliment, I don't need to say anything; my community will say something because we're one in the same. Throughout the years, we've had many trolls come in and say one-liners to make me cry or get under my skin. I come back with a better one-liner, chat laughs, and then that troll becomes a part of the community. They put down their guns and say, "I like it here!" I have a few viewers that started out as trolls and they've been with me for three or four years now.

LIVESTREAMER INTERVIEW: Sir Slaw (Twitch.tv/SirSlaw)

Q: What do you think of being considered an influencer? Is there anything important about this idea that you'd like to express to other livestreamers?

A: We all have opinions about this. It's a hot-button issue, and we'll continue to discuss it as our industry grows. I think the best way to approach something like this is not to be overly critical of people's decisions as influencers within these communities. But we do have to understand that, whether we want it or not, by sheer fact of being broadcasters on Twitch, we do have influence. We have influence in everything we do and don't do, what we say and don't say. I think, while it may not be our responsibility to tackle certain topics a certain way, it's our collective responsibility to be knowledgeable of what we say and do, and the impact that will have on people, the industry, our communities, and each other.

Leadership Reminders

There is no perfect formula for being a good leader. Every Twitch channel, livestreamer, community, and situation is unique and requires a slightly different set of skills or personalities to navigate. It generally takes people a lot of time and practice to figure out how best to create live content on Twitch, let alone how to foster a community for people that's also compelling to join. The best anyone can hope to achieve is to create unique content that's true to the creator and fun to watch and interact with for viewers

As you grow and learn how to lead your community, remember it won't always work out they way you plan it. People are complex, and livestream situations often require an understanding of human emotion and thought to guide and connect with people on a deeper level. And to top it off, leading others and putting yourself on public livestreams can also have negative effects on your physical and emotional health if you aren't careful. Here are some things to keep in mind:

1. No matter the situation, it's not your job to solve everyone's problems. It's easier than you think to end up being involved in other people's issues as you begin to establish friendships on Twitch. As a livestreamer and influencer, you will be asked questions, and viewers will share stories of their personal lives to get your opinions and advice on their situations. As they learn about and see your life via your livestreams, you will also hear about viewers' lives and their ups and downs. This is a great level of interaction—you can invest in others as they invest in you. However, this can lead some viewers to make assumptions. You are their friend and they know a lot about you, and they assume you know a lot about them. They may come to you for advice outside of your livestreams, via social media or on voice chat services for your community. They may send you messages on Twitch and expect timely responses to every inquiry. The more open you are to your community, the more open they will be with you, and at some point you need to set limits. While it's always kind to listen and try to help others, know that it's okay to say when enough is enough. If you need time away from viewers and responding to messages, it's good to say so and let everyone know that you won't be responding to messages until a certain date, or after a given number of days or weeks. It's also okay to tell viewers that you understand and hear their situations, but to a certain extent you cannot help. If viewers are going through difficult personal issues, it never hurts to encourage them to find professional help.

TIP: Interacting with viewers isn't always this intense, and it may never reach this level, regardless of your Twitch channel success. However, it's important to understand that a situation like this may arise. If it does, you'll be prepared to handle it accordingly.

2. You are not on call for viewers. We encourage you to make your content on Twitch consistent, as that's a key factor in growing your channel. That means setting a stream schedule that viewers can depend on.

This ultimately provides the greatest chance for viewership success. But aside from setting a consistent schedule and tone, you are not required to stream at the whim of your viewers. Life happens, and sometimes you can't keep to your stream schedule. Sometimes you'll just be tired and will need a day or two off. That's okay! Communicating with your viewers about these things can enhance their understanding of you, and including them in the channel's news and updates allows them to feel valued.

There are times you may want to run a new schedule by your viewers to see what they think, or if there is any feedback to take into account, but you alone determine the stream schedule. You'll always want to make decisions that have the best impact on viewership, which means translating individual feedback into a holistic stream plan.

Some viewers can become aggravated if the streamer can't keep a consistent schedule. This is exacerbated by Twitch's monetary factor—if a viewer has donated money to the streamer via donation links or Cheers in chat, then the viewer may feel entitled to a certain level of content. This applies to subscription tiers as well. It's also easy for viewers to compare content quality and schedules between different livestreamers, and they'll sometimes make their comparisons known to you. In short, some viewers complain if you aren't consistent or if they think you aren't streaming enough. This is where we again refer you to the Know Your Limits section. It doesn't do any good if you push yourself to stream and create content outside your limits—the quality will suffer and you will burn out before long. Consistency is a key factor in Twitch channel success, so if you establish a schedule that you can keep, one that works for you and your channel, then you should stick to it, regardless of whether viewers request otherwise.

Twitch streamers and their viewers' perceptions of them are similar to the differences between viewers' perceptions of movie and TV stars. A movie star's high-profile movies are viewed at specific locations, and screen time is limited to two or three hours at a time, often with a long wait before the star's next movie is delivered. A TV star's show delivers many hours of content to viewers in their own homes and on a consistent time line, either scheduled to air on specific days and times, or via on-demand streaming. Hence, viewers may feel more directly connected to TV stars than they do to movie stars. Now, take viewers' perceptions of TV stars and put the content on personal devices, such as PCs, tablets, or mobile phones, which are with viewers at all times. Add some direct, real-time interaction, and viewers lean even further into a perceived relationship that doesn't truly exist at the level they imagine.

3. Attitude sets the tone. As a leader of your channel, you can set the tone of your content and community by the attitude you display during streams. If you want to create content centered on positivity, then make a big push to discuss positive thinking and problem solving via the discussions with chat, and push for positive reactions to gameplay or creative content. Is your channel all about having fun? Then push your personality to the max. Get reactive and over the top in the gameplay and content you create. How about providing relaxing streams that facilitate deep discussions? Consider planning your content in advance to think through topics; pose deep, open-ended questions you'd like to discuss during your livestreams; and bring chat back into discussion topics if the conversation veers off course.

4. Many small leaders are better than one big leader. Leadership is hard, and it doesn't come easy. You aren't expected to be an excellent leader, or even a good one, especially when you first start out. Work closely with your mods and regular viewers to help carry the burden of leadership by setting a good example in your chat and community. Understand that as a Twitch broadcaster, you create influential content in some way, even if you don't realize it, and it affects people. What you do with that knowledge is up to you, so think before you act. Approaching a small situation in a decent, positive way can help influence others to think and act like that in the future, and it can set the tone for your Twitch channel.

LIVESTREAMER INTERVIEW: wgrates (Twitch.tv/wgrates)

Q: How do you respond to rude or intrusive chatters?

A: I'm pretty sassy when it comes to new chatters saying rude or insensitive comments, like stating that the chat is dead (no one is talking). It's a point of etiquette that I try to teach people when they come into my channel. In the case of having a "dead chat," we're pretty clear that having a dead chat isn't the best. We get it, especially when we're playing a game that takes a lot of focus. So, I'll reiterate that we're focusing on the gameplay, and chatters will come out in between battles if they feel the need to. When I'm able during the stream, I'll explain what's going on and what our strategies are, and if people have questions they can feel free to ask. In general, I'll sass people back and see if they stick around.

LIVESTREAMER INTERVIEW: Venalis (Twitch.tv/Venalis)

Q: Did you think about community foundations and goals when you started your channel?

A: Not in the beginning. The whole reason I started streaming was because I had to take medical leave from my job at the time. I had some paid time off and I was bored, so I started browsing Twitch and thought, "this looks like fun." So, for the next six months I streamed, and at the end of that time I realized I liked streaming a lot more than my previous job. I started full-time streaming right off the bat.

Getting into streaming was spontaneous, but as far as laying the groundwork for knowing how to build a community, I had already established some skills because I played MMOs for many years. In particular, I started a very successful guild on one MMO, and we ran multiple groups through raids and instances. We were a progression guild that was the "big brother" of the server. We'd help out smaller guilds that didn't necessarily have the talent or the know-how to take on specific bosses. They'd come to our guild and we'd send in officers to teach smaller guilds how to do things. I sort of translated this big brother-ness and growing it to me and my moderator team on Twitch.

Q: When you first started livestreaming, did you think much about becoming a community leader or what that meant?

A: No, I had no idea. I just tried to do it with the same philosophy I had when playing MMOs. Each and every guild is completely different; each has its own rule set, the way its officers act, its own atmosphere. I didn't worry about any of that when I started; I just tried to create a good atmosphere in my chat, my guild.

LIVESTREAMER INTERVIEW: Sir Slaw (Twitch.tv/SirSlaw)

Q: When you first started livestreaming, did you think much about becoming a community leader or what that meant?

A: Did I think about it? Yes. Did I have any idea what I was actually getting into? No, I had no clue. I've been learning a lot as I go, and I've looked into tons of analytics on channels about this. It's perhaps around the 100-120 viewer mark where a community-focused channel may change to an entertainment-focused channel to retain those viewers.

When I started streaming, I wanted to focus on this transition and how to keep the channel community-driven. In terms of being a leader, I knew that if I was going to be good at this, I would find out pretty quickly.

Act II: Establishing Your Brand

By now, you probably have some livestreaming experience under your belt. You should have a fairly good idea of what kind of schedule and livestream style works for you, especially for your particular streaming energy. Like any other skill that you focus and grow, you now understand the basics and know how to practice them, but you may be unsure of the next steps for moving to the next level. How do you continue to grow and differentiate your channel from the millions of other Twitch livestreams?

This is where we explore distinguishing your channel from all the others. In Act I, we focused on establishing some of the basics for your channel: its foundational pillars, the most important things to you, and the ideas you want to promote through your content. Now we need to craft these foundations and make them public-facing so others can see what you stand for in a cohesive way. When viewers first come to your Twitch channel, what do they see and what do they want to know? How can you show viewers what you're all about within just a few moments of looking at your channel? Whether you're offline or online, it's time to take your channel to the next level by defining and building your brand.

Building a brand is no easy feat. Entire companies are dedicated to the sole purpose of creating meaningful branding. There are myriad theories on how to create a brand with impact. Psychology and market analysis are considered in how a company brands itself and what that means to its target audience. A lot can go into a brand, and figuring out what sort of brand works for you, your channel, and your viewers is the next big step in your livestream career.

In this section, we explore the major assets and ideas you need to consider when you create your unique brand on Twitch.

What is a Brand?

In essence, a "brand" is simply something that tells us the source of a product. Where did this product come from, or who made it? What products, if there are many, does this entity make? Branding originated thousands of years ago with the act burning symbols into livestock to show who they belonged to, the literal act of branding an animal. While the term branding still adheres to the original objective—i.e., where does this product come from?—the term has shifted over the years and is now regularly viewed as a way to take ownership and enhance the audience's perception of a given product or service.

Branding is a fundamental part of business. Every company, sports team, and celebrity has a brand. If it's well executed, their branding becomes an intuitive way for people to quickly understand what that entity offers. Done extremely well, the meaning becomes memorable.

Branding has become a focus throughout the rise of social media influencers and content creators. What better way to differentiate yourself than to create a stylish symbol or catchy name for your preferred content platform? Why not create a color scheme to tie all of your art assets together, and display them on your Twitch channel? The most memorable content creators establish brands that permeate their social channels and the content they produce. Some brands are so well recognized that you know the brand before you even know the person creating the content.

TIP: You don't need to be a content creator or part of a company to create a brand. You can do your own personal branding exercises to define who you are to the public around you! Just doing some personal branding in your school or workplace can help you see how perceptions are formed, how you are perceived by others, and what you can do to adjust these perceptions.

You've seen millions of brands throughout your life, and some of the most effectively branded products stick with you long after you've seen them. Let's take Twitch's branding as an example.

Twitch's logo is well known throughout the livestreaming space, partly because it was the first successful gaming livestream platform, but also because of its simple characteristics. The deep purple color used in all official Twitch branding is widely recognized. The typeface, style, and design of Glitch and the Twitch company name is presented in such a way that it's easy to remember. Glitch, in particular, can provide insight into what Twitch finds important to express to its audience. A chat bubble shape filled with eyes—or quotation marks—can represent communication and speaking between people, a big factor for Twitch's interactive entertainment branding. It's simple enough to be memorable and perhaps repeated enough that people can retain the logo in their minds. The Twitch brand is so popular

that people purchase Twitch-branded merchandise. Being able to wear the Twitch logo on clothing is perceived as prestigious, which is evidenced by the long lines at TwitchCon merchandise booths and the desire to obtain the highly coveted purple and white hoodies that Twitch staff and partners wear. A brand is much more than a logo, font, and color scheme; it should support the message, vision, and goals for the company or person using the brand as well. Let's take a holistic look at how to create a brand for your channel, and what steps are important to consider along the way.

Creating Your Brand: First Steps

First, let's look at the elements you defined as the backbone for your livestreams from Act I. We'll call these your pillars, the most important things for you to strive for, and what you want people to know and understand about you and your Twitch streams. These are the foundations upon which you are building for your livestreaming career. What kind of streamer are you: high energy or relaxed and chill? What kind of content do you typically make: gameplay walkthroughs with tips and tricks, or reactionary gameplay videos where anything goes? What kind of environment and community do you want to foster: having good times and rolling with the punches, or really pushing for deep discussions with your viewers on a wide range of topics?

TIP: How you formulate your brand is up to you. The branding is strictly for your use and thus focuses on your likes and personality type. You can make a more general brand for the entire channel, which includes its personality and the type of environment or feel you want to create for your viewers.

At this stage, boiling down your pillars into keywords can be beneficial. This can help you hone in on the ideas you want to convey in your branding. Each pillar can consist of just one word, and you can begin to extrapolate additional ideas and themes from these pillar foundations. Let's try an example:

Stream foundation: I want my Twitch streams to be fun and relaxed, where anything goes and I have a good time sharing experiences with my community.

Pillar 1: Friendship

Pillar 2: Positivity

Pillar 3: Variety

If the three preceding keywords are the foundational pillars you want to stress to your viewers, then you can use these as a starting point to think of themes and messaging surrounding those ideas in your branding. Let's use the first pillar, friendship, as an example for brainstorming images and symbols, colors, messages, and features that we could use in a brand.

Images: What types of images or shapes could symbolize friendship? Circles, handshakes, and an infinity symbol may come to mind.

 Colors: What color do you think helps enhance the feeling of friendship? Perhaps a bright color, like yellow or green, could do the trick.

 Messages: What phrase or tagline can you use to further reinforce friendship? Let's go with "Support, unity, and happiness for all."

 Features: What do you want to do or show on your stream that supports viewers via this branding? Overlays that display welcome messages to new followers and subscribers? Emotes that viewers can use to say hello to other viewers?

Try following this process for all the pillars of your channel. This will give you a good base of ideas from which to expand, and you can reinforce the ideas by finding similarities, compatible ideas, and themes between them all. From there, you can build your brand, but know that this isn't the only way to do so.

You may start this exercise and realize it's just not working for your style. Or, perhaps you want to skip this step completely and just focus on coming up with ideas that are meaningful to you. There is no right or wrong way to work on your brand; do what feels right, and the more creative aspects will come with time.

Next, take a look at some of your favorite products and companies, along with their branding logos and campaigns. Try to determine why you like them. Does the color scheme call out to you? Does the tagline stick in your head? Make a list of what works and what doesn't from your perspective, and add those to your branding ideas.

Don't forget to take a look at broadcasters you enjoy watching and see what kind of branding they have for their Twitch channels. Define what you like about their branding, and take some time to list why. Does a nice logo make you interested in a streamer? Are the emotes alone compelling enough to have you join a channel or subscribe to the broadcaster? Are the channel's information panels set up and correlated in such a way that you find yourself interested in the content the streamer has to offer?

Defining and describing what you like about other brands can be one of the hardest steps in creating a brand of your own. Trying to define what works and what doesn't, and why, can be tricky. Then, applying these concepts to your own Twitch channel can take a lot of time and experimentation. Ultimately, your perspective isn't the only one that matters. Of course, you want to create a brand that defines you and your channel well, but it should also appeal to your audience. Finding a balance of your style, creating a brand you believe in, and creating something interesting and compelling to the audience is a challenge. It's okay to come up with many ideas and discuss them with your peers or community members, too. Sometimes decision by committee can reinforce your choices, or at least help you hone in on a few ideas, but sometimes it can lead to more options than you originally started with. If you decide to open up your branding ideas and decision making to a group of people, we recommend you narrow down the ideas to your top two or three selections. Keeping decision making within your confined parameters helps you focus the group on providing the right kind of feedback and answers for the proposed issue.

Once you have a solid idea of the kind of branding you want for your channel—a logo idea, some font and color themes, and key messages or catch phrases—you can put them all together for a first draft! Even if you aren't an artist, it's best to grab some basic shapes or stock images and throw them together in a document you can eventually pass on to an artist for logo creation. The better defined your brand is from the beginning, the easier it will be to communicate these themes to an artist or specialist who can create your final brand assets.

LIVESTREAMER INTERVIEW: Venalis (Twitch.tv/Venalis)

Q: At what point did you first start to think about branding for your channel?

A: Right at the beginning for the most part. When I first started streaming, I had no intention of using the logo and phrase that I use now. I originally had a bigger beard, and the small group I had suggested that I market the beard. So, my first few raids were "The Beard Raid!"

Maybe a few weeks into streaming, my fiancée asked why I was using the beard for branding. We had a great brand from a guild we had in the MMO we played years ago, and she suggested that I use that instead. So, we brought in the brand that I loved: Hail Darkside. I thought about it and decided it was a great idea. I found a sports logo designer and commissioned the Darkside logo, and I've been running with it ever since.

Q: How did you decide on your channel's branding? What steps did you take to define that brand?

A: Before I switched to Darkside, I did some research on Twitch. I looked at all the big streamers at the time, and I realized they all had that thing—that one phrase, that one logo, that one thing. And it clicked for me. Hail Darkside is my thing; I've always done that. It wasn't something that I tried to craft meticulously. It was something that I enjoyed over the past ten years of my life, when I played MMOs in my guild, and I wanted to share that with the world.

LIVESTREAMER INTERVIEW: LittleSiha (Twitch.tv/LittleSiha)

Q: How did you decide on your channel's branding, and what steps did you take to define that brand?

A: I try to have my branding fit what my channel is about. I love being happy and positive, so my logo and graphics are naturally very colorful. It's best to have your branding fit what you stand for.

LIVESTREAMER INTERVIEW: The Hunter Wild (Twitch.tv/TheHunterWild)

Q: At what point did you first start to think about branding for your channel?

A: Before I started streaming! I structured the nature of the stream that I wanted to create, the branding itself, and the business plan for it during three plane flights. So, the vision, mission, and branding all came to me within a few flights before I started streaming. The branding itself seemed very natural for me. "The Hunter Wild"—my name is Hunter, and it works really well. You can immediately conjure up imagery for this. An obvious theme for this shows up instantly, and it carries over into my identity as a person, and seems very fitting and fluid. A lot of people fantasize about getting back to nature and wilderness, and there are a lot of games around that too, so it made for a very obvious kind of fit. I imagine this is a pretty rare scenario.

Q: How did you decide on your channel's branding? What steps did you take to define that brand?

A: I could have gone with many other options; I didn't have to use my real name. I could have tried to structure some kind of branding on top of a different idea. I did, and still do, spend a lot of time thinking about the branding and how to expand the brand. Still, 9,000 hours and almost four years into streaming, and I'm still thinking about ways to roll out and make expansions to the brand, on what it is and what it could be, and that takes a lot of time and effort. Even if your brand is handed to you on a silver platter, you should still spend a lot of time and consideration on it.

Creating Your Brand: Advanced Steps

Develop your advanced branding assets to support and coexist with the basics: logo, color, font, and messaging. From this, you can create all other brand assets. Remember, now is the time to make your channel cohesive—the stronger the connections are between your channel display, your chat, and your content, the stronger your brand will be as a whole. This makes it easier for new viewers to remember you in the sea of Twitch broadcasters, and it provides veteran viewers a way to describe your content to others and help them promote you. The advanced brand assets you need for your stream include: emotes, panel images to display on your channel below your live feed, and onscreen scenes and overlays.

In addition to visual branding, you can also experiment with audio support, special events, and refining your on-camera persona.

Specific and directed audio can enhance your livestreams and create more meaningful ties to your brand. The sounds you choose for onscreen alerts and the music you play before and after your livestream can all factor into your branding. Maybe you have a funny quote clipped from a previous livestream, and you play that for every new follower or subscriber.

From how you handle onscreen notifications to what kind of special event livestreams you create, keep your branding in mind. Some streamers want to get their viewers excited when they receive donations or subscribers, so they may play a song and start dancing to the music to celebrate. Some streamers use face and body paint to write the names of new followers and subscribers on themselves during the stream. Regardless of what you do, you can consider doing special events for celebrating when things happen during your stream.

We all act differently in different settings, with different people, in different situations. Livestreaming is just like any other scenario. Chances are, you're being yourself on stream, but maybe you're just a little more formal than usual. Or, perhaps you react more openly to things during a stream. Or, perhaps you yell and curse and let yourself get into the gameplay you're displaying. There are bound to be slight changes in how you act and speak while you're on a livestream, but this doesn't mean you aren't acting like or being true to yourself. Defining this onscreen persona can support your branding, or the branding can help you determine how to act on stream. The caveat here is that you don't want to dive into a persona that's drastically different from who you are in real life, unless you have the determination and ability to carry that persona every time you stream for the duration of your livestreaming career.

LIVESTREAMER INTERVIEW: The Hunter Wild (Twitch.tv/TheHunterWild)

Q: What steps did you take to define your brand's persona?

A: My persona focuses on discussions and bringing thought processes out in conversations, and this stemmed from before I started streaming. I have a degree in philosophy with a personal focus on existentialism. I'm a philosophical Buddhist. People ask me all the time, "what's the meaning of life?" and my canned response is "co-creating experiences together and being with others." That's something I discovered awhile ago, and I found that livestreaming was a perfect fit for me because that's exactly what it is. It's interacting with people and sharing experiences on the biggest potential scale without sacrificing intimacy or personalization.

For branding the persona, it's the same exact reason I started streaming in the first place, and they became inextricable. Thank god for the internet, because now we can co-create experiences across any distance at light speed. I think this also ties back into the imagery for my branding. As inherently primal creatures, we emerged from the wilderness. Wilderness was one-and-the-same with humanity, and using wildness as a theme for us being together despite all the things that want to jump out at us from the darkness. We huddle around the fire and we tell stories and we create experiences together, and it works really well.

LIVESTREAMER INTERVIEW: wgrates (Twitch.tv/wgrates)

Q: Describe what your brand is on Twitch.

A: My underlying brand has always been corgis, overall. For my original channel panels on Twitch, I used stock images of corgis. My schedule panel was an image of a corgi with a book that said "schedule" on it in horrible blue writing. My tipping icon was a blue background image with a corgi face on it, with a name tag that said "Hatred" on it. This was because, in my channel, my currency was "hatred." There was a long-running channel meme that I accumulated long before I started streaming, which was "I hate you all," because I hate everyone equally! So, it was a random motto, but it was also a long-running joke because, if you took the time to get to know me, you'd realize there's no possible way I could hate you. I love everyone so long as they do right by me.

So, originally, it was hatred, which is completely contradictory to my current channel branding. Around September 2015, I started streaming more frequently.

I started dual-streaming *Warframe* with another streamer, and I was sort of jealous of the way she could interact with her stream because she had a camera on. At the time, I wasn't streaming with a camera. So, I looked around for a way to find this level of interaction without using a webcam, and I came across a program that superimposed a character over my webcam feed. One option was a dog character that I could stream as, and I said why not use this—let's just do it for fun! I immediately saw an increase in viewership. Within a month, I had a huge jump in viewership, and nothing happened except the addition of this character over my webcam feed.

So, I did that for a while, and nothing else changed on my channel branding. As more people started watching, my mods changed my commands to be more dog-focused, like **!pet** and various things like that. And then they said I should change my currency, and my channel went through a natural re-branding based on viewer and community feedback.

Now we work "the assistant" into it, which is me in person. We all know that I'm both the dog and the assistant, and we have fun with it. It's one of those worst-kept secrets, especially when someone asks how we do the animated dog onscreen. The community will respond that I'm a real dog.

Q: What were some steps that helped you define this as the right brand for your channel?

A: Community reception to a lot of these things was great. We just had a lot of fun overall, and the level of interaction it allowed me to provide for my community. The fun caveat from me is that I tell anyone who's thinking of doing this not to do it. The hard part with all this is you get into character and you make it you, but where do you go next? It greatly limits your ability to do anything else going forward.

This means streaming opportunities at conventions won't work, because you can't use webcams on your channel. Sponsorship with brands is very difficult; you can't do a little social media video with you in it, you can't wear T-shirts on stream, you can't drink or eat sponsored products on stream, you can't show off sponsored gaming peripherals or gaming devices. You pretty much shut those doors unless you figure out a way to do it. For this style of streaming, it needs to be all or nothing. I've seen some channels do it halfway and it just doesn't work to the same level. It doesn't feel the same.

I saw a popular streamer who also took on an animated dog persona on Twitch, and he tried to stream himself as a human, and his whole chat called for the dog to come back. Then his numbers dropped like a rock when he streamed just himself, and not as the dog. It's one of those things that you have to commit to. If you go this route, you're not coming back. And if you do decide to change from one style to the other, you have to be okay with losing some followers.

Q: Was the bigger impact on your brand your effort and hard work being entertaining, versus leaning on the art aspects of the brand?

A: One is the respect and integrity that my channel has overall. The openness, the friendliness, how I treat other livestreamers, and how I visit their streams is a wonderful part of it. My emotes are also very recognizable, and viewers use them in many other Twitch channels.

The branding really helps out a lot in keeping it all consistent. I had a solid community as a good foundation, and the animated dog and corgi branding helps a lot. The animated dog brings in viewers, but after five minutes it gets old. So, you have to keep thinking about how to keep viewers in the channel after the novelty wears off. And that's also where branding comes in.

Branding Emotes

We discussed what emotes are in Act I of this book. Now, it's time to create (or revise) your emotes to match your branding. This could be as simple as ensuring all your emotes feature the same art style or color scheme. It could be as advanced as redesigning the emotes entirely to facilitate the pillars of your brand and content. It could be adding a new emote that's a well-known joke, quote, or memory from your community. It could be a variety of these things, or it could be a mixed bag of images that are relatable to your viewers. No matter what, there should be some defining factor that bridges the gap between your emotes, your brand, and your livestream channel.

Onscreen Scenes and Overlays

It's time to revise your onscreen art assets to match your branding! You may have been using placeholder or pre-made assets on your channel up until now, which is a great way to start out. In fact, the assets you're currently using may already be a fine match for your branding. It doesn't hurt to review and revise the look of your live feed to match the look and feel of your brand, and you should conduct periodic reviews of your assets to ensure they don't go out of date.

There are many different options for stylizing your onscreen assets. Depending on the broadcasting application you use to stream, you may already have access to pre-made art assets that you can modify to fit your needs. Some programs provide full-scale themes, which can encompass pre-made art assets for a number of different scene setups and functionality. You can use them for onscreen alerts, moving ticker bars, full-screen images for end caps on your livestreams, and more. Themes are generally easy to install and reorganize to fit your content needs. Some programs also allow you to modify colors and animations for the different onscreen alerts, and can provide animations to transition between scenes.

Some programs don't come with overlay themes, but they almost always provide the ability to add and update your own media files to create overlays. These programs sometimes offer more flexibility for your livestreams, but can be overwhelming for a streamer who's just starting out with onscreen assets. Usually, when you use these types of programs, you'll either want to continue using preconstructed art assets, make your own art assets to fit your particular specifications, or enlist the help of an artist to make custom assets for you. Regardless of what program you use and how you use it, the underlying objective is still the same: produce art assets that conform to and enhance your channel's branding.

LIVESTREAMER INTERVIEW: Venalis (Twitch.tv/Venalis)

Q: Where do you feature your branding (in overlays, social media, etc.)?

A: I go through spurts of branding. Sometimes, I want to coast and focus on having fun on stream. Other times, I want to shotgun blast the marketing and branding everywhere. I have custom animations for going live on social media. I have branded merchandise. I have branded information panels. I don't add too much on my overlay, but I have an animated wallpaper, so whenever I talk to the stream, I have my animated logo on display. I try to push it as much as I can, as long as it's practical.

One thing I did in the past, when I first got the Darkside logo done, I was really excited to share it. I did a giveaway and said, "Get a Darkside shirt, and whoever takes a picture with the Darkside shirt in the coolest place gets a prize." That was successful, and we did another one later for taking a picture with the Darkside shirt in the largest crowd. Nothing obnoxious, nothing to troll people, but we incorporated some guerilla marketing techniques.

LIVESTREAMER INTERVIEW: The Hunter Wild (Twitch.tv/TheHunterWild)

Q: Where do you feature your branding (in overlays, social media, etc.)?

A: Interestingly, I think where and when branding is featured is sort of consistent with the brand itself. Speaking of the philosophy of nature, there's an interesting idea about the demarcation line between wilderness and non-wilderness. When we're really engaged, it's fluid. There's no tree line where you go, "Oh, there's the end of the farm and the start of the wild, and when I cross that line I'm in the wilderness." It doesn't really work like that as much as we might conceptualize it. There's a constant interplay there, and with the visualization of my brand, we have that sprinkled around all over the place in the same kind of way. It's maybe not intended to make you feel like you're in the woods in a fluid and natural way, but it performs the same kind of function because it's always there. There's no hard line for like, "now you're experiencing our branding visualizations." The visual themes are all across the board, sprinkled in.

Panel Information and Extensions

Panels comprise the information and images you present on your Twitch channel below your live feed window. Twitch offers livestreamers the ability to modify these panels by adding text and images to help brand and describe your channel's content. Some panels can display extensions, which are externally created apps that function for a particular purpose. For example, you can add a panel with a schedule extension, which will countdown the time to your next livestream.

If you use extensions on your channel, you'll notice that most don't provide a great deal of customization. Many are limited to a specific function, and often don't provide the ability to update colors or images within the app. This means you likely won't be able to update an extension panel to match the look and feel of your other branded panel images and onscreen overlays. Extensions have been growing in number and popularity in recent years, and it's believed that expanded functionality will be provided for extensions in the future. But for now, Twitch livestreamers have to use extensions in their current form, without major modification options.

TIP: Utilizing the same art style and color scheme between panels is a great way to create a unified front on your channel. Tying this in with onscreen scenes and overlays is an even better way to create a cohesive channel brand that can be memorable to viewers.

A best practice for panel images is to adhere to the standard Twitch image size constraint, which is currently 320 pixels wide. Images can be used as section headers and can also be linked to a URL. Or, the entire panel can be an image that includes branding and all the relevant text information.

Livestreamers usually display panels of information, including the streamer's biography, the stream schedule, rules for the channel and chat, community links to voice chat services or other community websites, donation links, social media platforms, special thanks, and chat commands. Twitch affiliates and partners usually provide subscription information, including links to subscribing to the channel and what benefits subscribers receive, as well as images of the unique channel emotes for subscribing.

LIVESTREAMER INTERVIEW: Sir Slaw (Twitch.tv/SirSlaw)

Q: Do you use extensions on your channel? Which ones?

A: I use only one extension for my channel. It's something that I and a few people on my dev team built. It shows all the people in chat currently, and whether they're a subscriber. You can click on their names and it will take you to the gift sub-page on Twitch. It's so simple, and I've gotten very positive feedback on it from viewers and other livestreamers.

Branded Merchandise

Outside of digital branding on Twitch, livestreamers can also add their branding to merchandise via external companies and websites. Some companies allow you to sell your own products, while others provide the manufacture of those branded products as well. Selling products on websites usually requires some percentage of the sale to go back to the company selling your products. In general, selling branded merchandise can take a lot of setup time and effort, so we advise you to leave this as one of the last steps after your branding is finalized. It also helps to establish your branding on Twitch first. Chances are, not many people will buy your branded merchandise if they don't know what your content is about or what you stand for.

Typical merchandise that some streamers sell includes T-shirts, hoodies, and stickers. Some streamers also offer cups and mugs, mouse pads, and pins. No matter what types of items you sell, make sure you have the legal license to sell your branded items. This means ensuring your artwork is valid for resale (meaning you created it or you hired someone to create it, and they gave you the rights for commercial use) and that your products are valid for resale (meaning you have the legal right to sell or resell your branded physical items).

TIP: Taking the extra care to review your licenses and agreements with artists and vendors is a critical step before you sell branded products. If you are ever unsure about your legal rights regarding artwork or manufacturing and selling products, please consult a legal advisor.

Depending on the type of branding you've created for your Twitch channel, you may find you need a simplified version for creating merchandise. We recommend creating a version of your logo that removes detailed line art and can be printed clearly in two-tone colors or in black and white.

The simpler you can make your logo for merchandise branding, the better, so your logo can be printed easily with just a few colors, without spending more time and money on multicolored print runs. A simplified logo is also more visible and recognizable from afar.

TIP: Remember, merchandise can be purchased and used by anyone. Don't put anything in your branding that you wouldn't want a wide range of people to see.

Staying Consistent

Everything should be coming together now. You know what kind of content you want to make, you know the brand messaging and logo you want to use, and now it's a matter of keeping it consistent. Easy, right?

This is where willpower, determination, and perseverance really kick in. Your on stream persona should match well with your branding and the content you create. It sometimes means getting mentally prepared in advance to bring a lot of energy to your livestream. It sometimes means preparing a "run of show" document beforehand to help guide discussions and plan for conversations with viewers. It definitely means keeping up with your stream schedule and making sure you alert your moderators, viewers, and social media followers when you'll be going live on Twitch, or when there is a deviation in your schedule.

Communication is important at this stage. Get engaged with your viewers and keep them updated on your stream status, and take into account their feedback on content. Want to try out a new roleplaying game? Ask viewers to vote on what RPG they want to see you play, or if they want you to continue playing the game you're streaming. Thinking of discussing a current event in the games industry on stream? Ask viewers the kind of questions they want to discuss. The more involved your viewers are in your streams, the more likely your channel is to succeed. Regular viewers tell their friends about your stream, and new viewers get interested in the level of dialogue you engage in with your chat.

Perseverance can be tough at this stage, especially if you don't see an increase in viewership, follows, or subscriptions. Even if the growth is slow, seeing some sort of progress can help keep you motivated. But what if you aren't getting many views, or your numbers are always the same? Well, consistency is good no matter what, even if your numbers have been the same for years.

There's no perfect formula to grow your Twitch channel. You've already taken a lot of great steps to make your stream consistent in branding and content, and you're putting yourself out there to lead the charge and foster a community of viewers. But if your numbers haven't changed or, worse, they've decreased, then maybe it's time to switch up the plan.

Keeping consistent doesn't mean doing the same ineffective thing over and over again with the hope that someday it will magically work better than before. Keeping consistent means making your planning and processes reliable. If you change your schedule hoping to hit a new audience around the world, then you need to be consistent in explaining to current viewers why you're adjusting the schedule, and be consistent in analyzing your post-stream data. If you want to switch to a game genre you've never played before, tell your viewers you want to try something new and get them on board! Viewers are understanding, but some come and go depending on how you modify your channel. Getting used to the ebb and flow of viewership can help you track what's consistent versus true increases or decreases in your numbers.

Change is inevitable, and it's better to welcome it and try new things on your own terms rather than get stuck in an unsuccessful rut. Be consistent and true to yourself while trying new things in a structured way. Analyze, adjust, and revise—for science!

LIVESTREAMER INTERVIEW: Venalis (Twitch.tv/Venalis)

Q: What do you think is the most important thing in branding?

A: Create and commit to something you can genuinely get behind for the next five years. Doing a total rebrand is very difficult. I've seen established livestreamers who averaged 500 viewers, who had been around for a while, and they just got tired of their branding so they went through a huge rebrand. And ever since the huge rebrand, they shot themselves in the foot and don't stream as much anymore.

Find a brand that is you. Market yourself, not a fake persona.

LIVESTREAMER INTERVIEW: The Hunter Wild (Twitch.tv/TheHunterWild)

Q: What do you think is the most important thing in branding?

A: We're still working on branding, even when it's so obvious and natural for my channel. Recognition first and foremost, and then beyond that, a sort of sneaky, parasitic infiltration. Can I get something into people's eyes and minds that, when they see something similar to it, they think of me and the brand and what we do? If you can present something thematically consistent and visually persistent—a mascot or a color scheme—that creates a unique combination that rides the line of standing out and blending in. That's the goal. That's what I strive for.

Q: What advice can you give to livestreamers regarding branding?

A: I've listened to a lot of people talk about branding, and I'm still not sure I really understand how to develop it. How to start from a blank slate and move from there to something you can actually use. I used to have a better idea. I used to be able to make a claim about this, but I've passed beyond that now. I recognize I was ignorant before, and I don't want to speak out of turn. I know there are a lot of things that I don't know, especially about branding. It's a strange thing, because it feels like an identity. With these kinds of things, we feel very intimately attached to them. Livestreaming isn't just a job, it's who you are. The branding is therefore an extension of who you are, your core identity, or at least that's what it feels like.

It's a very sensitive thing. We feel like everything hinges on whether or not we have a good brand. People go out of their way to get really good visuals, and they try to rebrand over and over again when they feel like it's not working. They feel like they're failing, and this is how they can redefine their identity in a controllable way. I wish I had a good answer for this.

In the end, make sure it has something to do with who you are. It will be hard for you keep up and connect with your brand if it doesn't feel like an extension of you. You need to commit to it and feel a commitment to livestreaming if you're doing it professionally. The brand should make a lot of sense in communication; it should feel like a natural fit whether you're talking to a community of people or a company of professionals. If you can't connect with your brand, it will feel flat.

LIVESTREAMER INTERVIEW: wgrates (Twitch.tv/wgrates)

Q: What advice can you give to livestreamers regarding branding?

A: Don't sweat your branding too much at the beginning. The most important thing about livestreaming is to actually do the livestreaming. I see so many new streamers going, "I'm thinking of starting to stream, but I just need to get my branding right first," and they forget that streaming means actually streaming and being on air. I made money streaming before I ever paid money to people for creating branded assets and emotes. I see streaming as something you do for fun and as a hobby until it can work itself out as a career.

LIVESTREAMER INTERVIEW: LittleSiha (Twitch.tv/LittleSiha)

Q: What advice can you give to livestreamers regarding branding?

A: Professionalism! Write any social media posts with proper grammar and punctuation, make sure any photos you post are high quality, and do proper promotion for your streams—post your schedule and when you'll be live. If I see a "Going Live" post that's riddled with spelling errors and full of a million random hashtags, I probably won't be going to that channel.

The Evolution of Your Twitch Channel

Like most things in life, your Twitch channel evolves over time. There are various reasons for this—you may get tired of or want to expand upon the type of content you originally made. You may come up with a great content idea while talking with your viewers and decide to begin creating that content. You may have an opportunity to make new content with other streamers or influencers. You may even be at static viewership and want to try something new to boost the numbers. Or, perhaps now you have more time and resources to update the kind of content you've always wanted to make.

Evolution can come in many forms, and much of it is within your control. You could rebrand to update all your panel images, emotes, and onscreen art assets, or even completely change the look and feel of your channel. Whatever changes you make to your channel at this time, consider your long-term goals and, in particular, what kind of success you're trying to achieve in your livestreaming career.

Defining Success

Before you buckle down and start creating your long-term goals, think about defining what success means to you. This will drive your goal setting in the near and long term. What does success look like to you? Or, what does it feel like? Too often, we define goals based on numerical values. This is especially the case with livestreamers, and the numbers are easy to compile and are key factors for determining Twitch affiliate and partner statuses, among other things. It's how most people measure what they consider top-level streamers; how many followers do they have? How many subscribers? How many times do they stream, and what's their concurrent viewership? How much money do they make? How often are they featured on the Twitch front page? Tracking numbers is pretty objective and clear, so it's tempting to define success through them. But to round out your goals, you should first define your objective and subjective success criteria.

Take some time to really think about what success means for you. Start with something basic—what's the most important thing for you to achieve in livestreaming? Write that down and expand on your success criteria from there. What's the next most important thing for you to achieve? Challenge yourself by thinking outside the norm, and limit yourself to just a few conditions for success. Try making one or two quantitative and the rest subjective.

TIP: Some of the most successful people of our time cite their definitions of success based on helpfulness to others, self-satisfaction, and overall happiness.

Let's run through an example to get you started. Perhaps the most important thing for your livestream success is the meaningful relationships you foster—be they with your viewers, with your mods and community, or with other livestreamers. Imagine you've also listed the following factors to achieve success: X number of followers and keeping to a regular streaming schedule. Wrap these up into a realistic time line, and you've set a definition for your success!

Example: "To me, success on Twitch means that I am streaming regularly on my channel, that I obtain 500 new followers within one year, and that I build and cultivate meaningful relationships with my moderators and community members."

Every person has a different definition of success. And, truth be told, one of the most important aspects of defining success isn't so much about achieving a specific numerical target. It's the matter of giving yourself a range to fall within, and defining criteria can help you make an action plan and set goals to fulfill those objectives. This is about you taking control and setting yourself up for success! One of the toughest things to remember and take to heart is the notion that just because some people believe that X number of subscribers means success on Twitch, that doesn't mean it's the only way to succeed, or even that it's the most important success factor. Once you believe in your criteria and set goals to achieve your own version of success, the more meaningful and fulfilling it will be when you livestream on Twitch.

LIVESTREAMER INTERVIEW: LittleSiha (Twitch.tv/LittleSiha)

Q: Regarding livestreaming, how do you define success?

A: When I first started streaming, success was definitely Twitch partnership. That was my end goal. That was when I was going to "make it." Everything was going to suddenly be easier when I got partnered. Wow, was I wrong. Partnership was only the beginning. Now that I've been streaming for about four years, success is being able to do this for a living. The fact that I get to do what I love every day and pay my bills with it is beyond comprehension.

Q: Do you have any advice for new or casual livestreamers on how to define success for themselves?

A: Whatever your goal may be, whether it's becoming famous, making lots of money, or just being able to play video games for a living, the best thing you can do for yourself along the way is to stay humble. If you act out, everyone will remember it: your viewers, other streamers, developers, potential business partners—everyone. Confidence will really help you in this industry, but arrogance will do the complete opposite.

LIVESTREAMER INTERVIEW: Sir Slaw (Twitch.tv/SirSlaw)

Q: Regarding livestreaming, how do you define success?

A: I'm a numbers guy—I'm such a data nerd. I love to test things. I love being able to analyze the numbers after a stream and figure out the topics during the stream and how they impacted chat messaging or viewer engagement. My definition of success is feeling like I'm having an impact with people, and the numbers really just help me understand that. So, to really get to the root of it, when I feel happiest and most successful with my stream, I'm not looking at numbers. It's when people make me feel I have an impact in their lives, and I can feel that repeatedly. If I have an impact on someone's life one time, that's fantastic. But if they come back to me three or four times over different conversation topics and they say "this is valuable to me," then that's when I know I'm being successful. I'm repeatedly bringing value to people.

Q: Has your definition of success changed over time?

A: Absolutely. I'm new to this, but when I first started, my definition of success was to get partnered, stream full-time, and get 15 people coming back every single day. We blew through those goals ridiculously fast. It's been such a wild ride that I haven't had a chance to reassess what I want to get out of livestreaming. Nowadays, success to me is starting my day in a bad mood but having my stream viewers cheer me up. I can afford to live and feed my dog; that's success to me. I'd love to blow up the channel and have an impact on ten thousand people, but at the end of the day I'm happy having an impact on people and living comfortably.

Q: Advice to new or casual streamers on defining success?

A: You really want to find your truth. I know that's abstract and very vague, and it typically goes in one ear and out the other, but you really want to find what speaks to you. I've always been an entrepreneur. I've always been interested in tech, and I wanted to build my own companies. I set some ridiculous goals, not even so much to hit those goals, but to figure out a way to build something myself. I think for most people who start streaming, they say they want to make money and have nice cars, but I think the root of it is we just want to build something and be proud of it. I think people need to be true to themselves and understand that's what they really want. They want to build something fun and great. Look past the perceptions and what the world thinks of you.

LIVESTREAMER INTERVIEW: missharvey (Twitch.tv/missharvey)

Q: Regarding livestreaming, how do you define success?

A: This is one of the biggest problems in streaming. As a livestreamer, you're never quite satisfied. You reach a milestone, and the next day you lose so many subs and so many viewers—always two steps forward, three steps back. It's really difficult to classify success.

If you can make a living off of this, that's successful. When you feel that your stream is always growing, that's success. Don't look at the day-to-day, look at the overall progression.

The hardest thing for me is the sub counts. They go up and down and up and down, and it's really tough. It can be disappointing and difficult to watch.

Q: How has your definition of success changed over time?

A: For me, my definition of streaming success was when I had over 500 concurrent viewers. I haven't had this number in about two years, since I don't stream full-time, and it's been frustrating. So, I changed my mentality, and now my stream is to give back to my community. It's not my job. I stream when I can to give back. It's difficult to quantify your success based on the reactions of others, so if someone tells me it was a good stream afterwards or they clip parts of my stream, then it was good. The numbers give more direct feedback, but I know the overall success is more complicated than that.

LIVESTREAMER INTERVIEW: Venalis (Twitch.tv/Venalis)

Q: Regarding livestreaming, how do you define success?

A: Being able to buy meat.

I don't even classify myself as successful. That's because I have impossibly high standards. I think I'm very happy, but I personally don't think I'm very successful.

I think a streamer hits success, financially speaking, when they have a solid bottom line that isn't going to waver. Right now, I'm relatively okay financially, but I'm on that cusp where it can sometimes get scary. It's rough. I would highly advise to avoid measuring your financial success; measure your happiness.

Q: Outside of finances, how would you define success?

A: Happiness. I'm a good, old-fashioned man, where if you can end the day feeling like you put in a good day's work and you made people smile, then it was a good day.

If I feel content with what I've done throughout the day, and if I've enriched some other people's lives. That's why I've stuck with streaming. That's the happiness that I focus on.

Q: How has your definition of success changed over time?

A: When I started streaming, it was all about money. It wasn't the idea of I'm going to make millions! It was the fact that I had six months of paid leave and full-time streaming. I was making more money streaming than I was getting paid at my previous job. At the end of those six months, I left that job and stuck with streaming. So, in the beginning I was measuring it as, "This is really fun, I'm making even more money than I was at my previous job, look how successful I am!"

Over the years, it's been less about financial-based success and more about determining how long I want to do this with my life. And the answer to that is as long as I'm successfully happy. It very much has changed from when I first started.

Q: Advice to new or casual streamers on defining success?

A: The kind of thing that has worked for me over the years has been to set myself an absolutely unrealistic goal. If you do this, then understand that you are very unlikely to hit that goal—go in knowing that. Go in having fun, go in guns a-blazing. One of two things will happen: you'll either hit much higher than whatever a conventionally realistic goal may have been, or you'll actually hit this incredibly unrealistic goal. A "shoot for the moon, land among the stars" kind of thing. It's the motto I've lived by for a while.

My first year of being partnered, I said I wanted to hit one thousand subs. Within one year, I hit 850 subs. I didn't hit my goal, but I was extremely happy with the result.

Goal Setting

If you haven't started thinking about them yet, it's time to define your short- and long-term goals for your Twitch channel and for you personally! The most obvious goals, or perhaps the easiest to define, likely involve numerics: number of followers, subscribers, and concurrent viewers. But contemplate the subjective long-term goals for your channel. What kind of content do you want to create regularly by a certain date, what personal skills or talents do you want to improve, and how do you want to feel overall?

Your goals should lay out milestones for directly achieving your success criteria. This helps you create a plan of action, but it doesn't necessarily mean if you hit all your goals, then you'll automatically meet your success criteria as well. There's some give and take—you may be achieving your goals, but what if they don't really align with your success criteria? Or, perhaps in six or eight months, you find that you need to readjust your success criteria, and thus your goals. The objective of goal setting is not to force you to adhere to certain things, but to provide the framework for planning how to achieve your own level of success. It's to put you on the right path. Nothing is certain in this world, and you can adjust your actions and perspective to put yourself in a better position for success through goal setting.

Setting goals may not be easy. Your success criteria may be a bit abstract, which makes it difficult to pin down realistic and measurable goals. That's okay! Starting with something abstract is fine, and you can (and should) continue to refine your success criteria and goals as you go. Even if your success criteria remain abstract, the key here is to make goals that are actionable.

You've probably heard of "SMART" goals, which is a commonly used acronym to describe the management practice of creating achievable goals. SMART stands for Specific, Measurable, Attainable, Relevant, and Timely. SMART methodology is the foundation by which you can create and compare your goals to see if they align with traditionally successful goal setting, and thus make them more likely to be met. Let's take one of our success criteria from the last section and create some targeted, structured goals.

Success Criteria: "To me, success on Twitch means that I am streaming regularly on my channel."

Goal setting for streaming regularly:

To facilitate ease of streaming, I aim to set up all of my stream equipment on the first Saturday of each month, run through tech tests, and ensure that no issues arise while livestreaming.

In the first two months, I aim to stream twice a week on Tuesdays and Thursdays from 6:00-9:00 p.m.

In the next two months, I aim to continue streaming Tuesdays and Thursdays from 6:00-9:00 p.m., and also stream on Sunday afternoons from 1:00-3:00 p.m.

In the last two months, I will continue streaming Tuesdays, Thursdays, and Sundays, and also stream Mondays and Fridays from 7:00-10:00 p.m.

As you can see, the goals we've created are specific; we know how often we want to stream for each goal, on which days, and for what specific durations. They're measurable and attainable. Be reasonable with your expectations, and make your goals difficult enough that you need to work to achieve them, but don't make them impossible. They're relevant; they feed directly into your success criteria of streaming regularly. And finally, they're timely; this means they're realistic and, in this case, adhere to a six-month time frame. This is enough to establish your streaming behavior and see results without reaching so far into the future that you feel like you'll never reach the end.

In general, the type of goal we used in this example isn't to be confused with your on stream or outward-facing goals. They can be similar, and sometimes the same, but generally your on stream goals will factor into your overall short- and long-term goals. An on stream goal is something you publicly announce as your goal on the stream. These can be goals that you speak about during the livestream or even display as a progress bar overlay on your livestream scene to show your progress toward hitting that goal. Showing goals can be an excellent motivator, not only for yourself (the incentive to hit goals rises as you make them publicly known), but also for your viewers. Viewers may directly impact your onscreen goals, like donating money to a charity for which you're fund raising. Other viewers may strive to publicize your goals to their friends and social media followers with the hope of motivating folks to help you hit your targets. Let's take the next part of our success criteria as an example.

Success Criteria: "I want to obtain 500 new followers within one year."

Goals for gaining followers:

On average, I aim to gain at least three new followers each time I stream.

To incentivize new viewers to follow my channel, I aim to always verbally acknowledge and thank them for following while I'm streaming. I will also play a song and do a fun dance to celebrate their follow.

To motivate current followers to share my Twitch channel and follower goals, I will conduct a prize giveaway when I hit 100 new followers. I will do this five times, and I will pull a winner from my channel's follower list each time.

To facilitate getting new followers, I will show an onscreen overlay that displays a "Follower Progress Bar." This will indicate how many new followers I have on my channel for a predetermined amount of time (e.g., per livestream, per week, per month, etc.).

You should plan your long-term goals six months to one year in advance. They can be great milestones for analysis and self-reflection. Are you on track for meeting your success criteria? Overall, are you happy with your livestream experience so far, or are there things you would change about your content, goals, and schedule? Are you seeing positive growth on Twitch and feel you're able to take on more of a challenge, or do you need to scale back and adjust your time commitment?

LIVESTREAMER INTERVIEW: Sir Slaw (Twitch.tv/SirSlaw)

Q: Do you set goals, and what kind do you set?

A: Yes, absolutely. I believe no one should put all their eggs in one basket. My goals have always been to diversify. I want to build my channel, but I spend a crazy amount of time off stream working on tools for broadcasters and viewers. Building things to make people's lives better. In the end, I just want to improve lives. Every goal I have for myself revolves around bringing more to the table for people.

Q: Do you make any public-facing goals and display them on your stream?

A: I'm a big fan of social accountability. I feel like when you put something out in public, you're much more inclined to do it, or at least attempt it. I make public-facing goals around my channel's content, or something my community wants or needs. And sometimes it's stuff where I feel like I need to stand up and have a voice for people. I've recently set a goal for putting out more content to motivate people. Things to make others feel better. Social accountability is very powerful in helping any of us achieve our goals, or at least stick to them.

Q: Do you have examples of when a goal wasn't working well for you, and you adjusted it to better fit your situation?

A: I'm a firm believer in "failure is the best way to learn." So, I frequently make very lofty goals that are probably not possible, but some of them I've surprisingly met. Sometimes they work out and sometimes they don't. I feel that you learn best from failure.

For example, I just talked with my stream about some new goals. This month, I'm going to stream 300 hours, then 400 the next month, then 500 hours the month after that. I realize that's almost 17 hours of streaming a day. I'm never going to hit that, but I'll be damned if I don't try. I'm going to put forth the effort, and I'm going to learn a ton about streaming and my own breaking points. Things that I need to learn if I'm going to do this full-time. And one of the best parts about approaching things like that, as a content creator, is your community and viewers love seeing that story and seeing you grow. It's very powerful.

LIVESTREAMER INTERVIEW: LittleSiha (Twitch.tv/LittleSiha)

Q: Do you set goals? If so, what kind do you set?

A: Yes, absolutely! I love setting yearly goals for myself and making pretty graphics for them, so I can print them out and keep an eye on them all year round. For instance, one of my 2018 yearly goals was to get a Collector's Card with Twitch. Seeing that goal in front of me every day was a great motivator to get me to reach out to the right people and put my name forward.

Q: Do you make any public-facing goals and display them on your stream?

A: Occasionally, I'll do a sub goal for special events, like the anniversary of when my channel got partnered. However, I find it too intimidating to have it up all the time. I want my stream to be very clean and relaxed, so it's rare that I break out a displayed goal.

Q: Do you have examples of when a goal wasn't working well for you, and you adjusted it to better fit your situation?

A: I don't really have any examples of this because I tend to set my goals lower. I set lower goals because the more easily attainable they are, the more likely people are going to contribute. I think it's smarter to start lower and extend it once you hit that goal.

LIVESTREAMER INTERVIEW: missharvey (Twitch.tv/missharvey)

Q: Do you set goals, and what kind do you set?

A: I used to set public goals, but I haven't done that in a long while. When I was streaming daily, I'd put a 5/5 sub goals progression bar. I think it encourages people to sub and help me reach my goal.

LIVESTREAMER INTERVIEW: Venalis (Twitch.tv/Venalis)

Q: Do you set goals, and what kind do you set?

A: I set absolutely unrealistic ones. I always aim for the stars. I think this is healthy, but only because I have a healthy mindset about it. I know I'm not going to hit these goals. I don't apply this rule to other people, necessarily, since not everyone has this kind of mindset.

Q: Do you set numerical goals, or do you set other goals?

A: A lot of my goals are numerically based, but not all of them. An example of this is, years ago, I attended my first TwitchCon. I knew nobody there. I was not partnered yet, and I knew absolutely no one. I met big streamers and "fan-boyed" a little. I left TwitchCon that year and said, "By next TwitchCon, they're all going to know me."

Over the next year, I spent a good amount of time networking, joining their communities, hustling. I attended events that other streamers were attending. Then, by that next TwitchCon, I felt like every time I turned a corner, I had people coming up and saying hi to me.

Q: Do you make any public-facing goals and display them on your stream?

A: Very rarely. I did that recently for the first time, actually. There was an update to the Twitch emote tiers, and to test it out, I put a sub count goal display on stream to hit a certain number. I rallied my viewers and we hit it.

I rarely put these up on my channel. I'm too respectful, I think. I don't like putting goals up on stream. My community has already done so much for me, and I don't like taking advantage of them, as that's what it feels like. It's like setting an impulse buy at the counter of a retail store—you know they're going to buy it. But my community isn't a bunch of random customers. I'm not going to treat them like that.

The only front-facing goals I have are at the beginning of the year, when I say I want to hit a certain number of subs by the end of the year. I also do a once-a-year fund raising stream to attend TwitchCon. That's it.

Q: Do you have examples of when a goal wasn't working well for you, and you adjusted it to better fit your situation?

A: Not really, but this is because I set those really unrealistic goals. For example, the 1000 subs within the first year goal that we didn't hit, but we got 850 instead. My community asked what we were going to do for next year, and my response wasn't to still hit 1000 subs. It was to hit 2000 subs! We'll make up for the lost time throughout the year, it'll be fine!

For me, I've never really adjusted goals or compromised them. I don't really care if I hit the goal or not because I purposely set a goal too high.

Conventions

One of your goals may be to attend livestream events and conventions. Whether you're gearing up to meet viewers and other streamers in real life, make business and game development contacts, or preparing to go to your first convention ever, keep a few things in mind to maximize your time while traveling.

Plan ahead: Every convention provides a few aids to help orient con-goers. Get familiar with the floor map; create a rough schedule for your days, including meet-ups and panels or events that you want to attend; and know where you're staying and how to travel there and back from the convention venue. Preparing these things in advance will ease some of the anxiousness, and it will let you enjoy and remember your time at the convention.

Keep up the energy: Remember to take care of yourself! Eat enough to keep up your energy at a convention. You'll burn more calories than usual by getting up early, staying up late, walking around everywhere, and interacting with lots of people. Take breaks from the convention hall and people if you need time to recharge, as being in large groups of people for long periods of time can be difficult and draining.

Stay healthy: Let's say it again—remember to take care of yourself! Quite often, people who attend conventions bring home an illness. Take plenty of Vitamin C and keep up the cleanliness. You'll most likely shake hands and touch game controllers and merchandise items around the convention hall, which are great ways to pick up germs. Trust me on this one; you don't want to bring home the con plague.

Make connections: Whether you're at a convention specifically to meet viewers or other livestreamers, or you're just there to enjoy the event, it's best to come prepared. Bringing business cards that provide your name and Twitch livestream channel can go a long way toward people remembering you from a convention. It helps if these cards are designed such that their messaging and branding aligns with your Twitch channel. As you'll likely meet many people throughout one convention, it's a good idea to also write down information you want to remember in the moment. For example, directly after meeting someone, take a quick note of their name, Twitch channel, and something you spoke about—it will go a long way toward remembering that person after the event.

TIP: It's also a good idea to follow up with people you interact with after the event. Your message doesn't have to have anything substantial in it, just a quick "hello, it was a pleasure meeting you at X convention" can suffice. Take a few minutes to send them a note via email or on social media—they'll appreciate it!

Create content: Conventions are unique, and while you're there you'll have the opportunity to make some unique content! This could be as simple as custom social media posts—pictures from the event, selfies with broadcasters or community members, and daily recaps to let your viewers attend the event vicariously. Or, if recordings are more your style, you can create solo videos or team up with others at the event to make short movies or vlog-style videos for your sites (including uploading these videos to your Twitch channel via the Video Producers - Premieres feature). Depending on the event and your travel tech setup, you may even be able to livestream on Twitch directly from the event!

TIP: Remember that if you decide to livestream at a live event, you'll need to get permission from those you record on-camera.

So many conventions and events take place every year, and it can be difficult to travel to more than a few. Take some time to research the events and determine which ones you should attend in order to achieve your specific goals.

You can also create content around different events without physical travel. Some events provide livestreamed content, such as press conferences, which can be re-captured and streamed on Twitch channels. You can use this content to watch and discuss new announcements and updates with your community. Or, you can record reaction pieces to those updates and announcements. This way, your content is unique as it pertains to the information being released from a convention.

LIVESTREAMER INTERVIEW: missharvey (Twitch.tv/missharvey)

Q: What advice can you give to livestreamers who attend events and conventions?

A: Streaming-wise, try to book time to stream at the event. Since you won't be streaming like you normally do, just being at the convention may hurt your numbers but it will help your networking. So, try to stream from the hotel or the convention floor if you can.

Setting boundaries with fans and community members is important, too. Have ways to disconnect or close out conversations by shaking hands and thanking folks for their time. It's not healthy to just hang out with your fans, unless you're at a specific fan meet up or a community dinner event. Don't blur the line with people.

Utilize your convention time wisely. Now I prepare for conventions beforehand; I schedule social media posts, my schedule will be set well in advance, and I promote where I'll be and when. This is something I learned over time, and I attended so many conventions in the past that were a "waste of time" because I didn't plan ahead. As a streamer, there are so many things you can do to increase your reach, your stream, your time, and efficiency. Also remember to schedule some free time to relax.

Q: Do you attend events with a goal in mind?

A: I try to always have a meet-and-greet event whenever I'm at a convention. I try to associate it with a booth or a sponsor if I can. And even if only three people show up, that's great! That's a success. It's good to recognize that your community is so much more important than you think. No matter what my success is, if I don't have a community that follows me and clicks on the things I post or shares what I'm doing, then my work means nothing for sponsors or making a difference in society. You need a community, and you win them over one by one. Each person is valuable.

For me, this is really important. I've done so much in my career, from books to TV interviews, to documentaries, to competitions and conventions, and still to this day there are people who don't know who I am—and that's okay. I need to reach these people one by one, by attending another conference or by doing another book, or whatever. Even if someone talks to me for two minutes at a convention, that short interaction matters.

At some conventions, I hire an assistant to help me handle my schedule. I invest so much into talking to people that I lose track of time and I get really stressed. My assistant helps me with time limits, reminders of upcoming appointments, and getting from place to place. Most importantly, this allows me to dedicate all of my time and energy to interacting with people at the event.

LIVESTREAMER INTERVIEW: The Hunter Wild (Twitch.tv/TheHunterWild)

Q: Have you been to conventions before? If so, what kind of advice can you give to livestreamers?

A: You can personalize your convention any way you want. Currently, I have a manager who will be on the show floor and meet with contacts, discuss ideas and pitches, while I sit back and relax. Now, that sounds like a privileged position, and to some extent it is, but I have come to the realization that I would do this now, regardless of whether I had management. The reason is because I get so much more out of interacting with people on a personal basis during a convention.

What may be good for the business is not necessarily good for the brand, and what's good for the brand can overpower what's good for the business. Treating it like a retreat from the business side of things can be very valuable. You can see your friends and just hang out with them. For me, I'm a hermit streaming all the time; this is a once- or twice-a-year thing that keeps me going, and it develops the relationships that really matter in the long term. The people who, when you're down on your luck, will carry you forward until you can get back on your feet. That's way more valuable than whether or not a particular brand is going to make a deal with you.

At the same time, you can easily manage both of these things. If you're really good at it and structure it a certain way—get in, spend a certain amount of time on the show floor, and hit the booths you want to hit. Know where you want to go, give yourself a timer but don't check your watch, and nail those discussions. Do that job, and then make sure you spend some time with the people who matter—and not just at parties—spend time in quieter places with deep conversations. Get a lot of sleep. Drink a lot of water. Bring business cards. Have a plan, and nail it!

Q: What advice do you have for business card etiquette?

A: Have someone else check your business cards before you hand them out. My manager says to put as little as possible on your business card. I completely agree, and that's not how I do it. I'm really bad at it. I want to put a ton of stuff on my card.

Think of it like a pocket advertisement. Your name and contact information have to be on there. It has to be memorable. It should have a limited amount of information on it so the person knows what you do and what you're about. And some nice visuals—you don't have to include your branding, but maybe the visuals on the card tie in with your brand overall. It has to connect you with them.

Q: Additional advice on how to approach conventions and events?

A: As a smaller broadcaster, you're probably working a job and streaming. Use conventions to really connect with people and find time for yourself. Make the most of the events that you travel to.

Set up a good work-life balance. Much like any relationship, you can end up resenting your stream because of the amount of time and commitment you put into it. Very few of us get as much out as we would like. But in the meantime, I have to see various iterations of that value. I have to get more out of it than just the business side. And that happens through the day-to-day interactions with everyone.

If you don't love being with the people in your channel, then you're in the wrong career. But you have to have various versions of that. Nothing replaces the face-to-face interactions. For different people, it can have different iterations, but it's incredibly important to have that kind of interaction at least sometimes.

Q: Do you attend events with a goal in mind?

A: I used to have a goal. I tried to do everything all at once, and I ended up miserable at every convention. I'd get little sleep because I was trying to hang out with everyone at night, and tried work the entire floor during the day to do the business stuff. It was a killer. Now I go to a convention and I simply spend time with people that matter to me. People matter, it's why you stream for people, and that's really the goal.

LIVESTREAMER INTERVIEW: LittleSiha (Twitch.tv/LittleSiha)

Q: What advice can you give to livestreamers attending events and conventions?

A: Protect your health. I cannot count how many times a year I've gotten sick just from being at a gaming convention. Take vitamin C tablets regularly the week before, bring hand sanitizer, and make sure you drink plenty of water. It only takes that one handshake with the wrong person to put you out of commission for a week.

Other than that, this is a great opportunity to meet your streamer friends in real life and make new friends!

Q: Do you attend events with a goal in mind?

A: Honestly? Not really. Conventions can be really stressful, so I use them as a way to check out games I've been wanting to play and spend time with my friends that I only get to see a few times a year. That way, if I meet other streamers or developers, it's completely natural and doesn't feel forced.

Q: For someone trying to grow their livestream channel, what do you think is the most important thing for them to keep in mind regarding conventions?

A: Don't try too hard. It will come off as really uncomfortable and awkward. Wanting to grow your channel is a great way to stay motivated, but understand that it will also happen with time and patience. Keep it friendly with the people you meet and don't spend too much time talking about numbers.

LIVESTREAMER INTERVIEW: wgrates (Twitch.tv/wgrates)

Q: Have you been to conventions before? If so, what kind of advice can you give to livestreamers, specifically those who don't stream with webcams or use animated character overlays?

A: It's really hard. This was one of the main reasons why I finally put my personal picture out there, so I could show my face at conventions and people associate me with my channel. It's a blessing and a curse. You can walk around a convention and not get hounded by people, but at the same time no one will look for you because no one knows who you are.

General advice is to make a good business card that has your Twitch information on it. If you don't use a webcam and no one knows who you are, at least the card will point them in the right direction. Streaming without a webcam nowadays is pretty common. Having an animated character is a lot more common as well, but it's still so much harder to make that connection in real life.

It's also great to practice meeting people at conventions, especially in making business contacts with companies and game developers. Set your expectations as well; not every company will want to work with you.

Q: Do you attend events with a goal in mind?

A: I usually have one or two booths where I want to get in and talk with the game devs. At E3 this year, I made a few contacts for some future games and events. Again, you need to set your expectations and goals, and poke and prod at it from different angles. If you go up to one person working a booth, and they can't put you in touch with a PR person, then come back a couple hours later and ask for that PR person again. You never know which will work out, so you might as well keep trying.

Q: Have you created unique content while at an event?

A: I streamed at E3, which is one of my biggest highlights. I was really happy for that opportunity. I'll be streaming from the Twitch booth at upcoming events. It's a step up every time, at every event. I've started doing panels at events now, where I talk about working full-time and streaming full-time and what that takes. This is defined as 40 hours of work a week at my day job, plus two hours of commuting to work, and then I stream 28-32 hours minimum. I love doing this panel because it takes my experiences and the experiences of the other panelists and puts it out there to everyone who's looking to make streaming into something. Even if it's just for fun, we talk about tips and tricks and time management, and how to handle real-life events and a stream schedule.

Q: For someone trying to grow their livestream channel, what do you think is the most important thing for them to keep in mind regarding conventions?

A: Have fun! I say this for anything to do with streaming. If you're not having fun, then it's just another job. Do you really want to work another job? You're probably streaming to start doing it semi-professionally. So, have fun, that's initially why we all got passionate about gaming and streaming.

Relax a little bit. Just take it one step at a time. Don't be afraid to go up to people at conventions and strike up a conversation. Conventions are some of the best places to grow your stream professionally, because you can make contacts with so many game developers. I end up with 10-15 appointments with people before I get on the show floor.

It's also very important to meet other livestreamers face-to-face. TwitchCon is the best place to meet your peers, and it is a great event for community. Other events can be more business-oriented, but TwitchCon is where you can have fun, meet people, and hang out.

Off-Stream: Working Overtime

It's tempting to think most of the work for broadcasters happens during the stream, but that's where they're just getting started! Full-time livestreamers spend countless hours outside the stream working on their brand, communities, content, and analyzing stream data. This off-stream work draws a big distinction between casual and career livestreamers.

It's a telling sign that someone is dedicated to their craft and their community when they continue to think about how to make things better, more streamlined, and more impactful. This doesn't mean that everything can or should change, and especially not all the time. But the notion of never getting too comfortable and being open to change gives some livestreamers an intuitive advantage over others. If you hope to take the next step with your channel, then this is the way to go.

Prepping and Planning

Performers often say the key to a good performance is to practice and prepare. The same goes for livestreaming, and it's up to you to determine how you prepare and what's best for your channel.

Carving out some time in your schedule to get ready before you go live is a great way to prepare. You can spend this time reviewing and testing your technical setup so you don't hit any snags during the live event. Update drivers, check your lights and cameras, and monitor your PC settings (if you aren't streaming directly through a console).

Review your scenes, make sure your overlays are accurate, and all transitions work appropriately. Ensure each scene pulls the correct video and game data. Check your onscreen text for typos or missing links. Make sure you can switch from scene to scene without issue.

Prepare a short list of discussion topics in case there's a lull in chat. Did you read something interesting recently that you want to discuss? Is there a fun or compelling story you can share with your viewers? Or, perhaps you've had some time to think about previous stream discussions and you'd like to share your opinions or revisit old topics for further exploration? Having a short, bullet-point list can keep you prepared without straining your brain trying to remember all the small details during your stream.

If your livestream setup is complex, consider making a checklist of technical run-throughs to do before you go live. Remind yourself to do even simple things, like sharing your stream link on social media. Check that your microphone and webcams are turned on and working, and it never hurts to ensure your chroma key on the green screen looks good. Double check that the games you will be playing are loaded and ready to go.

Finally, remember to mentally prepare. Regardless of your stream style, being in the spotlight (literally and figuratively) can be draining. Keep your energy up by getting into the right headspace before you go live. Take a few minutes to meditate and center yourself, or listen to some epic music to get your blood pumping. Mental preparation for your livestream can make a big difference in the quality of content you present. It can impact your interactions with viewers, and it can keep you streaming for longer periods of time.

Clips, Highlights, and Collections

Soon after you conclude your stream, it's wise to review your broadcast and create any highlight clips to save to your channel. What happened during your stream will still be relatively fresh in your mind, so it'll be easier for you to find the clips you want to save. You can also enlist the help of your moderators and viewers to create clips of great content while you're streaming. Clips are excellent ways to show off your content and personality, and you can easily share them on Twitch and via social media.

Broadcasters can also create longer highlights of their previous streams. Or, the footage can be downloaded, edited, and re-uploaded into shorter videos that you can categorize within the Collections section of the dashboard. Use Collections to your advantage, and let viewers find the content they want as easily and quickly as possible. An easy way to create a Collection is based on the game you play during the stream. But you can also make Collections for discussion topics, or even broader Collections based on game genres or special events.

Updating Stream Assets and Bots

If you use third-party bots or tools to support your channel, periodically update them based on recent content you've created, such as clips, Collections, or full livestreams. Update your commands to state the latest information, or change your in-chat bot games based on recent discussions you've had with your viewers. Do you have a great clip that a viewer just made for your channel? Create a new timed command that sends out the link in chat every once in a while. Small adjustments and updates can make it much easier to keep your tools current for your viewers, and they'll lessen the workload later if you decide to do a major overhaul of your systems.

The same principle applies to updating and fine-tuning your on stream assets. You may love the overall look of your overlays and assets, so reviewing them with a critical eye very few weeks may be all it takes to keep things updated. You could reach a point where you want to create many different kinds of assets, either depending on your brand, the genre of game you're playing, or a specific game title you'll feature in upcoming livestreams. Revising these assets can take a very long time, and you need access to the programs for updating them, such as video- or image-editing resources.

More recently, third-party companies are creating bundled asset packages you can purchase and use on your channel, which is an excellent alternative to making your own. Of course, you can always commission an artist to make custom stream assets for you. It all depends on how much time you have and how often you want a fresh look for your livestream.

Analyzing Statistics

You'll want to dedicate a lot of time to analyzing your previous livestream performances. In particular, get familiar with the Twitch analytics and summary reports provided after every livestream. Some third-party tools and websites also provide livestream analytics, so it's all about what information matters to you and how you want to use it to track your growth. It may not sound very glamorous (and for some, it can be daunting), but this is an integral part of understanding your viewers and how your channel is performing.

Let's start with some quick and easy numbers to review. As you're livestreaming, you can keep an eye on your current viewer number, either through your streaming program or via the Twitch website or mobile app. This real-time number can help you derive some quick information. How many of your current viewers are chatting? Did you recently get a big spike or dip in viewers? Given any strong changes in your current viewer count, should you rekindle a previous talking point or start a new discussion to get people talking in chat?

After your stream ends, review the Stream Summary page on Twitch to understand what your average viewership was throughout the stream. Twitch provides details such as average viewership and when your peak viewership occurred. Now, with this time line and some upper and lower peak numbers, you can review the stream video provided by Twitch to discern what you were doing, saying, and what chat was talking about throughout the stream. In particular, you can see when viewership or chat interactivity spiked. Finding common threads through these timestamps and numbers can give you good insight into what your community enjoys, and you can generate ideas to replicate your success on future streams.

You can review tons of different statistics for your stream, not just those concerning current viewership. Look at where your viewers are coming from and which channels they're watching. You can track how many of your viewers were chatting on your streams versus the total number, and you can set goals for getting more viewers to begin chatting in future livestreams. You can spend a lot of time and energy reviewing statistics, but the time is well spent. Look for correlations and think about what you can do to influence the numbers.

LIVESTREAMER INTERVIEW: Venalis (Twitch.tv/Venalis)

Q: How much off-stream time do you spend on working your channel?

A: My fiancé says too much, I say not enough.

When I think of work, this includes every time I type Twitch.tv into my browser. Whether I'm in a friend's channel watching their stream, or I have an editing program up and I'm working on assets, or I've just ended my stream by putting together a compilation to reveal, or I'm in my Discord channel, or I'm doing movie nights with the community. I do all sorts of stuff off-stream, and I'd say it's just as important, if not more important, than your actual livecast.

If I stream for six hours a day, I'll put in four hours of pre- and post-stream work.

Q: Do you spend more of your off-stream time working on a particular aspect of your channel?

A: It really depends. Now, typically I spend all my off-stream time on my new animated intro. This includes face lifts to the logo, 3D rendering, highlighting, you name it. Whenever I don't have a big project like this, my typical pre and post work is focused on networking or hosting community nights.

Q: How much time do you spend on clips and Collections?

A: Depends on how good of a day it was. There are some days where you have to go scavenging because maybe the couple people who are clip masters weren't there that day, so you have to make some of your own. Sometimes, you can just look through your top clips of the day and pull the best ones. Sometimes it's fast, and sometimes it takes hours to put it all together.

Q: What do you think is beneficial about clips and Collections?

A: Recently, I've started pulling clips to use on social media. It takes time to download the clip, edit it to the specifications needed for the platform, and then upload it from there. I'm using them more for social media impressions—getting likes, retweets, etc.

LIVESTREAMER INTERVIEW: missharvey (Twitch.tv/missharvey)

Q: How much off stream time do you spend working on your channel?

A: I don't spend much time working on my channel outside of streaming, perhaps just 10 minutes before the stream to set up and recheck everything. Because I'm not a full-time streamer, my priority isn't to grow my channel or improve it every day; it's to turn it on, game, and win. I know my community, and I know what they want to see. Five years ago, I would have spent at least 30 minutes a day to go over everything and find ways to increase viewership and check off items on my streaming task list. I don't have that anymore. I've already cultivated my community, and now my streams are about giving back to them. My community loves my streams, even though I think it's very time consuming. They love it more than my social media posts, more than my videos, more than anything else. For me, streaming is just a way to give back to them.

LIVESTREAMER INTERVIEW: TheMavShow (Twitch.tv/TheMavShow)

Q: How much off-stream time do you spend working on your channel?

A: Every other waking hour. Is that too extreme? I spend a minimum of an hour before and after streams to make sure everything is set up and ready to go, and to post follow-ups and summaries.

Q: Do you spend more of your off-stream time working on a particular aspect of your channel?

A: The heart of it. I try to do more things in the world to have more to talk about during streams. It's great to stream crazy hours, but at the end of the day, in my experience, it's been great to spend a day or two a week just going out to have some inspiring conversations in real life, then bring that back to the stream.

Q: How much time do you spend on clips and Collections?

A: It really doesn't take too much time, and it's definitely something streamers should be doing. If you stream 5-10 hours a day of content in whatever field you choose, it's crucial to make clips and highlight what you've been working on. You should also go back and add each broadcast into a Collection, and keep all those files and hours of work saved.

Not everyone will sit in your channel for even an hour, but your audience loves you, so you should give them ongoing and extra content. Collections are a great way to do this, and they can also be great for audience members who may not have been with you for years and years. This way, they can go back and enjoy past broadcasts!

Q: What do you think is beneficial about clips and Collections?

A: It's an amazing way to share and get your stream out there, and even for you to see the fun moments you provide as a creator. It's easy to forget how entertaining or fun you're making things. There are times that I even laugh at myself when I watch these clips. Clips are great for sharing, and Collections are so helpful for organization and archiving.

Social Media Outreach

Why is Social Media so Important?

This question comes up frequently when discussing brand and what it means to be your brand. Often, it's not quite clear to the broadcaster that there is no "off" time for a brand, even if you're taking some time to be off. It's confusing, but don't worry; the explanation will make at least a little more sense. If you have a secret identity somewhere that in no way can be traced to your Twitch persona, then don't worry about this. However, short of that very unlikely situation, you are connected to your brand at all times. This means everything you post on any social media, any public face anywhere will become part of how the public and your fans see you. This isn't meant to pressure you into being someone you aren't; we're simply informing you that if you act a certain way on your broadcast and you act a completely different way everywhere else, it can be confusing to your audience. It can be harmful if you promote a positive and friendly stream in which you wish to attract viewers who are polite with each other, but you are rude or otherwise don't abide by your brand on other platforms. Having an inconsistent brand pushes communities away and makes it difficult for you to grow because, more than likely, your followers will not mesh well together, which can break apart a connected fan base.

Secret Identity

Many broadcasters keep their identities fairly secret and secure. More often than not, a broadcaster's name becomes public, but as long as you keep your address, phone number, and other sensitive information secret, you can stay protected.

Some broadcasters develop a character that's far enough detached from their real persona that it adds an extra layer of security to their information. This is almost never the primary reason to create a character on Twitch, but it's a great way to keep things hidden, especially your face if you use software like FaceRig, or you don't use a camera at all.

Explaining that it's difficult to keep your brand consistent might not be the most obvious way to illustrate the importance of social media outreach, but it's an important aspect to discuss before we describe how to positively affect your audience. Through interaction, keeping your audience informed, and maximum live time relevance, you can keep your brand solid while gaining maximum exposure. The constant struggle to stay relevant can be exhausting. You can try to keep up with the masses if you wish, but this chapter explores how to maintain your exposure efficiently and not burn yourself out.

Interaction

Interaction comes in many forms, especially through social media. On Twitter, you can like, retweet, retweet with comment, or comment directly on a tweet with words, emojis, GIFs, or photos. On Instagram, you have a slightly smaller arsenal, but you can still fully interact with anyone you follow, follows you, or whoever the media algorithms throw at you. It tends to be tougher to engage people on Snapchat and other lower-interaction mediums, but it's not impossible, and there's never a bad reason to spread your content to as many platforms as possible, if only to see what catches. The one thing to remember is that, the wider you and your brand are spread, the tougher it is to develop your brand as an interactive one.

Posting on multiple platforms simultaneously is becoming easier every day as one company connects to another and they offer options to share your posts to all of their platforms. Some users develop a rhythm that gets one thing posted to as many places as possible, as quickly as possible. Just because posting across platforms is becoming easier doesn't mean keeping your brand consistent has become easier. In fact, these integrations and advances have made it more difficult. If your posts are spread out and you wish to interact with the people that respond to them, you have to split your attention across all platforms, possibly repeating the same or similar thoughts. Specific users tend to stick to one platform and use it as their primary source of interaction. If you look at Twitch as your main platform, and Twitter, Instagram, etc. as your social media and external interaction platforms, many might interact with you on one or the other. Thanks to this somewhat tiered system, those folks have to take an extra step to get involved with your brand. The likelihood that most of your followers are willing to do extra work outside of watching you on Twitch is very low, but the odds of following you on one of these social media platforms is much higher. So, if you post the same thing to all platforms and someone asks a question about the post, you can answer them there, and many of your followers or viewers may see your response, thus mitigating the number of repeat responders to the same question or comment.

Repeat queries will still occur, but they will be less frequent. Now, if we look at methods to mitigate having to repeat yourself in order to keep your followers from feeling ignored, you're already doing a decent job by responding to at least the first few comments you see on a given post. Most folks understand that you simply can't answer the same question over and over, and they can refer to previous replies. This is a process, and interacting with your community definitely helps you get closer to its members; but remember, you made the same post on multiple platforms. Now, you must go to every other platform and perform a similar process in order to maintain the same brand. So, being aware of where your brand exists and where to pay attention is key. If you choose to develop a brand, it's important to be consistent on all grounds.

It's also important to note that every social media platform has a different purpose, and it's sometimes more efficient to consider which platform suits a specific post best and post it there. This can help you avoid spreading your brand too thin—you make the conscious choice to avoid spreading the widest possible net. As unintuitive this sounds, a slow and steady, focused spread of your brand can prove extremely beneficial in developing its consistency. Next, let's explore the sorts of posts that fit each type of platform.

Social Media Tips with Lowco

Q: How do you use social media to support your livestream?

A: I mostly use Twitter, as it's very useful in letting people know you're going live and networking with other streamers and developers. Of all the social media sites, I think Twitter is the best for streamers. I have my Facebook page synced with my Twitter, so tweets are automatically replicated onto my Facebook page. I use Instagram for pictures and sometimes even stream clips.

Q: How is social media best used during and immediately around a livestream?

A: You should definitely be tweeting whenever you start up your stream. Include the game you're playing, a brief description of what you're doing, and tag the developer or publisher too; you never know if it'll grab the attention of the community manager! If you're switching games midstream, definitely tweet again to remind people you're live and to potentially draw in new viewers.

Q: What are some tips you would give to broadcasters to help them protect their privacy whilst using social media?

A: Try to make sure your social media handles match on all platforms, and just be careful with how much information you share about your life. For example, if you go to a local coffee shop, it's not a good idea to share the name of that shop if you don't want people figuring out where you live. So, avoid specifics about aspects of your life and think before you tweet.

Social Media Platforms as Game Genres

If you imagine each of the many social media platforms as a different video game genre, it may be easier to compartmentalize how to use each to its utmost utility. Of course, you should develop your own method, but following are some examples that can get you started.

Twitter—First-Person Shooter (FPS): Tweets are short bursts of information often intended to hit targets from short and long distances, but they are almost always meant to serve a single purpose. Sometimes they're jokes that miss the mark by a mile, which can either yield a dud tweet or be so hilariously off target that they create a splash and bring your followers together to laugh with you. There's also the occasional explosive tweet, which is akin to a well-placed grenade or perfect headshot. These can also bring everyone together to cheer alongside you and your accomplishment.

Instagram—Role-Playing Game (RPG): Thanks to the introduction of stories on Instagram alongside normal posts that scroll down someone's feed, two forms of imagery or video work on this platform. Similar to an RPG, you are given long- and short-form elements to look at in order to get an idea of what's in front of you. Use Instagram to give people context into what's going on in your stream via a clip or image from that stream. If you look at the description of a character, item, or locale in most RPGs, it usually contains an image or video, and it's paired with either a short or long description that tells you everything you need to know right then and there.

Snapchat, Facebook, and Tumblr: These three platforms fall somewhere between Twitter and Instagram. If you think of Twitter as *Call of Duty* and Instagram as *Dragon Age*, you might think of Snapchat, Facebook, and Tumblr as hybrids, such as *Elder Scrolls Online* or *Battlefield*. They're RPGs, massively multiplayer online (MMO), and/or shooters of some kind. They attempt to accomplish multiple things at once. And, as in the gaming industry, they must do these things almost perfectly in order for them to succeed. This also means you have to post to them perfectly to be successful. Hybrid genres are geared toward very specific audiences, and they often aren't quite as big as the focused genres, but they're still worth playing. The same applies to Snapchat, Facebook, and Tumblr. You should still post to these platforms, but if you just don't have time to keep up with them, you'll merely lag behind in the fairly limited arenas that their extremely dedicated users support. Meanwhile, you can focus on doing what has proven effective for you in the two major fields, such as Twitter and Instagram.

Keeping Your Audience Up-to-Date

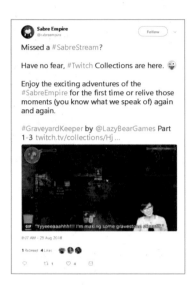

Keeping your audience updated may not be the most important part of learning how to use social media effectively, but it is a legitimate use of the medium's tools. With the introduction of extensions, Discord, Skype, and the Twitch app, there are many ways for your community to stay current outside your stream. The problem with relying on social media that are server based or require an invite is users have to put forth additional effort to join the community. Social media platforms like these are ideal for those ready for a deeper level of interaction with you and your community. Thus, keeping this audience up to date is relatively easy thanks to the dedication it already possesses. The challenging part is keeping newcomers informed to further sell your brand to them and entice them to return after their first or second interaction with you.

It's very important to keep newcomers interested in your show and your brand, as they are the easiest viewers to lose. However, keeping your regulars up to date is even more important because they care more about the future than they do current events. New members have a ton to learn about you. Of course, new members also want to know what's in store for the immediate future because they're interested in what they're signing up for. In order to satisfy and inform both parties, it's smart to post information regarding both the near future and news that might be further out. You may not have full details for either, but it's good to at least discuss what may happen instead of keeping those who care in the dark.

Like everything to do with social media and entertainment on Twitch, you want to post things at similar times throughout the week, preferably when your stream would normally be live. People are creatures of habit, and although your community may reside all over the map, members learn your habits and do their best to keep up with them. Why not make it easy on your followers by posting your channel updates around the same time each day, or at least the same times as you have in the past? You don't have to be obsessive here. If you get ready for your stream close to the same time each day, this might be a great opportunity to write a quick update on your social media accounts. You can also use third-party schedulers that post updates for you as long as you remember to schedule them.

Maximum Live-Time Relevance

If you've taken some time to observe your favorite Twitch broadcasters, you may have noticed a few standard practices. Maybe you've seen clips in which the broadcaster did something noteworthy or extremely entertaining, or maybe something is captioned just perfectly. Clips make great posts for showing off your stream, especially when you're offline. You may have seen posts about interesting or inspiring interactions that broadcasters have had with their communities on stream. On Twitter, many broadcasters replace their display name with something to indicate they are currently live. The great thing about the display name is that it updates live globally. Even if you look at a post from several months ago, the name you see above the post is whatever the account holder sets as his or her display name in real time.

All of these strategies are great for spreading a broadcaster's brand, but these posts are much more effective when they're posted while the broadcaster is live.

If you consider that almost every broadcaster posts to social media when they go live to alert their followers, you might wonder about others who use social media at other times. Of course, you don't have to watch Twitter every moment of the day to see older posts, but unless you scroll through your time line to see everything since your last check, there's a good chance you'll miss quite a bit that was posted earlier. This is where we circle back to our point about not burning yourself out on trying to reach every single follower by posting something every waking moment. It's good to stay relevant, but there are ways to be more efficient.

So, you've started your broadcast and you've made your social media posts to alert followers that the show has started. If you've been consistent with your timing, there's a good chance the people who can watch the show will arrive and check in. However, chances are your followers don't always tune in the very moment you go live. You receive followers throughout your active stream and sometimes when you're offline, so it's beneficial to post more than once while you're live. If you're comfortable using a post scheduler, that's the easiest tool to use while you're live; it allows you to pay attention to your broadcast 100% of the time. For example, you can schedule a simple post, like, "I'm still live, and we're playing *Fortnite*." Straightforward posts inform your followers who may have forgotten you were going live. If you take a two-minute break between games every few hours to post a clip to social media with a caption about what's happening, you can show your followers what they're missing. This can remind them why they followed you in the first place, and they'll more than likely check into the broadcast, especially if you make it clear you're still live.

It's hard enough to encourage your followers to join your stream amongst the many others on Twitch. It's even harder to get people to join you for the first time—the only tools you have within Twitch are the game you're playing, the title that's shown to the public (which is only 33 characters until viewers go to your channel), and the small chance the front-page system recommends you. Thus, you should use all the resources the internet has to offer, and social media is one of the most powerful tools in your arsenal.

Off-Stream Optimization with Lowco

Q: How much off-stream time do you spend on working your channel?

A: I spend an hour or so in the mornings before my stream and a few hours in the evenings after my stream each day.

Q: Do you spend more of your off-stream time working on a particular aspect of your channel?

A: Reading and responding to emails, social media, and schedule planning all take a good chunk of my time daily.

Q: How much time do you spend on clips and Collections?

A: I personally don't spend too much time because my moderators help me out, and my community is really good about capturing clips! I just need to make sure I encourage them to clip the best moments of the stream.

Q: What do you think is beneficial about clips and Collections?

A: Clips are fantastic for sharing on social media—and potentially having it go viral— and for showing community managers and viewers what you're all about. Collections are helpful to organize video content that you'd like people to watch again later. For example, videos of an episodic series.

LIVESTREAMER INTERVIEW: LittleSiha

Q: How do you use social media to support your livestream?

A: Relying on your streaming platform alone for discovery is not enough, so social media is crucial to getting new people in your channel. I use social media to let people know when I'm going live every single time. I also use it to promote any bigger streams, such as charity fund raisers or sub-a-thons, well in advance so people can be prepared.

Q: How is social media best used during and immediately around a livestream?

A: Right before I go live, I will post a "Going Live" notice as a signal to let people know they can come hang out. If I'm live for an extended period of time, I'll usually either bump the same post or post again to let people know I'm still live for those who may have missed the original notice.

Q: What are some of the most effective posts to define your brand?

A: For me, the most effective posts are photos. If I'm going live, it will usually be a GIF from one of my streams or a photo from any convention I might have recently attended. It's much more eye-catching than a post without anything visual to go with it!

Networking Is Not a Dirty Word

Networking can be a divisive concept. Or at least it can seem that way, given many people have a negative reaction to the word. But networking isn't a dirty word, and it shouldn't be considered a bad practice, either.

At its core, networking makes connections and brings people who share similar goals and interests together. It's the process by which you find and cultivate connections to people with whom you share information. It falls into the same realm as negotiation; it can be a bit daunting, and the negative connotation is the thought that you're trying to get something out of someone or that you're trying to swindle another person. In reality, negotiating and networking can benefit everyone involved. No single party needs to get substantially more out of these practices than any other.

TIP: Networking sometimes gets a bad rap, which likely stems from the fact that some people are bad at networking, have had bad experiences, or are intimidated by the process. Everyone has their own goals and agendas, wants and needs, benefits and strengths. To enhance your networking experience, think about how your pitches are perceived by others—tap into the benefits that others receive by being your contact and doing business with you.

Meeting through friends, family, and colleagues is an excellent start to networking for your career. If you're introduced to others by trusted people in your field or social circle, then you're more likely to be trusted by association. It can give your networking a boost, but it doesn't mean you have to work through your friends or colleagues to make connections. In practice, surrounding yourself with good people who you believe in and trust leads to connections with other trustworthy people.

It's important to understand that networking works best when the ideas you discuss are beneficial to everyone involved. Your ideas are better received if you take other people's goals and concerns into account. For example, if you go to a convention with the goal of meeting big livestreamers and pitching a charity stream that needs their involvement, then come prepared to make your case in terms that appeal to them. Explain who you are, what your channel is about, the charity event's goals, the type of publicity you want to generate, how their participation can make this a unique and successful event, and what benefits they receive from working on this idea.

Actively networking in person at events or online through Twitch is one of the best ways to find business opportunities, sponsorships, and collaborations with other livestreamers and game companies. Having a healthy amount of energy and enthusiasm for networking is great, but keep in mind you can fall into bad networking practices. Just as you can probably tell if someone is interacting with you just to get something out of you, so too can others see that about you if you try too hard to get noticed while networking. Be honest and transparent about your intent, and understand that you don't need to hustle for connections 24/7 to achieve the level of success you desire.

Networking Online and in Person

As a broadcaster, a big part of your off-stream work will be networking with others online. Making genuine connections via the internet can be a challenge. It's harder to convey your authenticity and intent through words alone, especially if you've just started a connection with someone new. So, how can you show others that your intentions are good, and that collaborating with you can be meaningful and fulfilling?

TIP: Remember that Twitch livestreaming revolves around creating communities and experiences together. If you want to make lasting connections, start by joining other livestreamers' channels. When you take a vested interest in others and their work, it goes a long way toward showing your commitment to knowing and working with them.

If you're networking with other streamers online, then you should dedicate time to watch their streams, talk with their communities, raid them to bring in new viewers, and host their content on your channel. Do all of this without asking for their return investment. If you're generous as you build up trust with others, then your real, heartfelt enthusiasm will transform your cursory connections into friendships over time. This will lead to business and streaming opportunities down the road and, most importantly, authentic connections with people around the world.

Networking in person can be similar to making connections with other streamers online. However, you should take timing into account, and that will impact how you approach these situations. For example, say you're at a three-day livestreaming convention. Let's imagine your goal is to meet at least four other streamers and make at least one business networking connection. Because you have a goal in mind, you can plan how to approach the event and determine the strategy you will use to meet people and network throughout the convention.

Timing is a big factor. In our example, you have only three days to make these connections, and only a handful of minutes to make a good first impression upon meeting them. Come prepared with information about who you are and what your channel is about. Provide your business card so they know how to reach you, and ask for theirs in return. Be real when you speak with them about your community, your channel, and your goals. Discuss some ideas with them if it's appropriate within the time they have for you, or just get some face-to-face time with them as a real person and not the persona behind the stream. Use your time wisely. If your contact is surrounded by people, then get in for an introduction but don't take up too much of his or her time. If they look stressed or busy, ask to follow up with them after the event to continue discussing ideas.

Not everyone will be receptive to networking or business pitches. There are many factors to take into account, and just because something doesn't work out the first time, it doesn't mean it can't work out with the next person, or even the next time you talk with that same person. Learn from your experience and utilize that knowledge to understand how to better network as time goes on.

Twitch Teams and Peer Support

As you navigate the waters of Twitch livestreaming, you'll start to build a core group of streamers and connections you can rely on for insight, analysis, peer review, and feedback. The sense of community and helping others is one of the greatest things about Twitch broadcasters. Livestreamers aren't afraid to talk about their experiences on Twitch and, more often than not, they're eager to share their best practices with others. Something that didn't work well for you might work extremely well for someone else in a different situation, and vice versa.

Networking with others can lead you to opportunities to join livestreaming teams. Each team is different, but the general concepts are similar. Teams tend to have standardized ways of supporting their livestream members. Each person gives something to the team, and in return all team members benefit from cohesive management and a unified front.

Regardless of whether joining a livestream team is right for you, understand there are pluses and minuses to joining a team. It may mean that getting business deals and sponsorships becomes much easier, but it could also limit the types of companies that you can work with. Joining a team allows you one more way to stay relevant to other streamers and viewers. You could also gain more networking power on a combined team than you have as a lone streamer, and it could greatly expand the types of pitches you can make to companies, thanks to the diverse set of streamers within the team.

All in all, the connections and friendships you make through online and in-person networking far outweigh the business contacts you make with companies and game developers. Cultivating the connections you make with other broadcasters is of paramount importance, and it's the most rewarding in the end. These connections can always lead to more business opportunities in the future.

LIVESTREAMER INTERVIEW: Venalis (Twitch.tv/Venalis)

Q: Do you have any networking advice for livestreamers?

A: At events, keep these things in mind: be respectful, don't be shy, and be professional. Every person I met for the first time at an event, I made sure I looked nice and was on my best behavior. Have a good time, and don't fan-boy too much.

Networking on Twitch can be very difficult. It's tough to try to network online without trying to "dirty network." So don't do it. Instead, become a part of people's communities. Every single streamer I look up to on Twitch, I join their channels, I sub to them, and I talk to their viewers. I actively watch them when I can.

LIVESTREAMER INTERVIEW: TehMorag (Twitch.tv/TehMorag)

Q: What are your thoughts on networking?

A: Networking can sometimes be confused with friendship. Or, to some people, the words can be used synonymously. I think the big thing with networking as a whole is setting expectations.

Make sure the people you're talking to know what your expectations are as well. It'll make you look better, you won't look "leechy," and it sends a clear message about who you are and what you're trying to do.

Nobody wants someone who feels like they're being buddy-buddy and then suddenly they go, "Hey, I see that you stream! Do you mind raiding or hosting me?" Instead, how about this: "Hey, I really enjoy your community. This is who I am, this is what I do. You should come by and check it out. And hey, maybe a raid or a host—we're very open and welcome these kind gestures from other communities. It might be something you're interested in."

Some people would still frown upon the second approach, but honestly, be up-front with people. That's the best way to network. If you want to be friends with someone, let them know. If you're trying to expand who you are, let people know who you are to try to broaden your horizon. Let people know up front, hands down.

Q: What if someone responds negatively to your networking?

A: If they don't like it, they don't like it. You can't change them. If you feel your honesty about what you're doing will offend someone, then that person may not be who you're looking for within your community, because they're not willing to be honest. If they realize what you're doing, as an individual, they'd at least give you the time of day and not be rude to you. If they're just rude, then I don't think they're someone you want to be around.

A no-reply isn't a bad reply, either. Let's say you send a private message to someone, and if you don't get a reply from them, don't worry about it. Try again in a week or two. If it's something very important, then try again in a little bit, but don't spam it. And there's a difference between networking and soliciting.

Q: At what times are you networking with others, or how often?

A: I'd say that within my stream, word of mouth, and social media posts, I do that a lot. Outside of the stream, I used to do a lot more. I need to do a lot more. I used to do easily two or three hours a day making sure I stayed in contact with people I knew, saying "hi" in other chats, and writing emails to different companies.

Q: Do you think spending time in somebody's chat and with their community can be useful in networking?

A: That's what most people are actually doing, and they don't even realize they're networking. It's being aware, and you could confuse networking with staying relevant. How many people know about you? By going into other people's channels and talking with them, you'll stay relevant.

Q: Do you have any networking advice for livestreamers?

A: Stop trying so hard. If you try too hard, people will see it. Don't be a machine, don't be forceful. It's not bad to show you're working really hard, but when you communicate with people, give some leeway. Make sure there's an understanding and set those expectations.

Here's an example of mine: the first convention I went to, I ordered way too many business cards. I still use them to this day. I went to a Twitch panel when Twitch wasn't very big at the time. And, at the start of the panel, I ran up and down the aisle and talked with anyone—everyone—to try to strike up a conversation. It was one of the hardest things I've ever done in my whole life. Even to the point where a big streamer told me a couple years later, that he saw me handing out my business cards to everyone at that event, and he was wondering who that jerk was. I remember also running to the door after that panel and handing out my business cards to everyone exiting the panel room. Nowadays, that would be extremely frowned upon. That's solicitation and you might get kicked out of a convention for that. When I did it years ago, I was right on the edge of whether it was acceptable or not. But at its core, you want to find ways to get out of your bubble and be relevant to people.

Twitch Programs: Affiliate and Partner Programs

Programs to Strive For

Why do you hear every broadcaster talk about the affiliate and partner programs? A lot of broadcasters use them to categorize each other. If you ask any broadcasters worth their salt how these programs differ, they'll usually explain that there isn't much of a difference; those in the affiliate program just haven't hit their goals yet. Many folks seem to feel the need to compare themselves to others. These designations have some uses, but unless you use them for legal reasons within the Twitch platform or you need specific perks from the partner program, there really isn't a reason to worry about which label applies to a given broadcaster.

Getting Started

If you're just getting started on Twitch, maybe you have no idea what these programs are, so you obviously aren't part of either one. That's absolutely fine—this isn't a race.

Twitch Affiliate Program

The Twitch affiliate program came along much later than the partner program. It's intended to help broadcasters monetize their channels quite a bit faster than they could before, at least through first-party means. If you're just getting started as a Twitch broadcaster and maybe you've never streamed, or you have little experience, this program is something to explore.

The affiliate program is great for broadcasters learning about monetizing their channel, but some broadcasters who have been in the program a long time feel affiliate status is too easy to attain. Not only is it too easy to attain, they reason, but it can also be difficult to reach the next stage, Twitch partnership. They might feel stuck and unsure what to do in order to advance. When you get the email invitation to the affiliate program, you receive a few perks. These help you understand first-party monetization methods. Before you join this program, please read and review the contract before you sign it.

Perks of Being an Affiliate

- Your channel gains a "Subscribe" button, which allows your viewers to subscribe to you for $4.99 per month, or for free with Twitch Prime.

- Your subscribers can use one emote per tier subscription they pay for. You are allowed one emote per tier, so making great emotes is very difficult but important.

- Your channel is allowed to receive Cheer or Bits from your viewers. Cheer can be purchased from Twitch, and each Bit used on your channel translates to one cent.

- As an affiliate, you join a priority list to receive transcoding on your channel. This means anytime you're in the top percentage of streamers—often this percentage is near the top 50%, but this is unconfirmed—your viewers can adjust the resolution quality at which they watch your stream. It can be difficult to watch streams that lack this feature, as viewers must then use the broadcaster's native resolution; a slow internet connection can spoil this experience.

What You Need to Become an Affiliate

You can track your progress to the following goals on your dashboard's Achievements page.

- Reach 50 followers

- Stream for 8 hours

- Stream on 7 different days

- Reach an average of 3 viewers

Twitch Partner Program

Many broadcasters aspire to join Twitch's partner program. For many, reaching partnership is the beginning of a professional career on Twitch. As we explain in the Streaming as a Career chapter, we happen to disagree. You can begin a career on Twitch at any point in your broadcasting experience—you are the determining factor, not an arbitrary label. That said, the partnership program offers broadcasters a platform with a lot of support. At conventions, partners receive special access and may be treated a bit differently. But realistically, any professional in the industry who treats others with respect can be treated this way. Partners receive expedited support when their channels experience problems. However, if your channel suffers a technical issue, chances are, the same thing is happening site-wide. The following partner perks are visible to your audience:

- You receive emote slots based on your highest subscriber count. On your dashboard, you can see your total subscriber points and your progress toward a new emote slot. You need a lot of subscribers to reach the maximum number of emote slots, so you are always encouraged to grow.

- Your channel receives a checkmark next to your name, which shows the public that the platform designates you a verified and trusted user. If you so choose, you can also display this checkmark by your name in any channel in which you chat.

- You can save your previous broadcasts as videos for an entire month longer than other Twitch channels. This allows your audience to go back to much older videos and catch up on them.

- You receive automatic transcoding on your channel every time you stream, regardless of the circumstance.

- You can periodically run ads on your channel while you're streaming, and you then receive ad revenue for the ads your viewers see. You can also choose to hide ads from your subscribers.

Following are some of the metrics Twitch uses to track your eligibility for partnership. Note that achieving certain targets does not guarantee you a spot in the program. This can be a point of frustration for broadcasters; some wait months after submitting a partner application only to be rejected. The affiliate program substantially increases the number of partner applications Twitch receives, so backlogs occur from time to time. The good news is that Twitch provides a set of milestones to reach before you submit an application:

- Stream for 25 hours

- Stream on 12 different days

- Average of 75 viewers

The first two targets are formalities, but averaging 75 viewers is a much more important goal. Twitch prefers to count your channel's native viewers, not viewers from hosts to your channel, so keep this in mind when you consider submitting an application.

Streaming as a Career

What Defines a Career?

What is a career? Can it be defined as something you're serious about? Something you've been doing as a job for a long time? Something that makes you money and provides a way to sustain a lifestyle you enjoy? Really though, which is it? Truthfully, a career is all of these yet none of them when you consider the Twitch space. There's no way to be very successful and make a career out of streaming unless you are truly serious about it. Streaming for a long time can be applicable here as well—if you consider the brief period that Twitch has been around as an industry, a long time might amount to only about a year or more. Consider that by no means would one year qualify as a career in many other industries, but most industries are far older. You should also note that, as you make a career out of livestreaming, you likely will not make anywhere near the money you could make in another job, at least in the beginning.

It's very common for Twitch broadcasters to make absolutely no money in a single month, but the same goes for starting your own business in any industry. Most business owners don't take a salary for the first few years after starting their businesses, even if they're more successful than the average start-up. The same may apply to your streaming career. This is one of the few industries in which most beginners start with zero intrinsic audience appeal and have to grow it from the ground up. At least in the restaurant industry, arguably one of the toughest industries in which to start a business, you know that people need to eat, and there's a quantifiable chance that people will pass by your restaurant, even in the most crowded city. On Twitch, if you aren't careful and you stream a game that already has a thousand or more streamers casting it, the chances of your channel being seen, let alone clicked on, are far closer to zero than any restaurant.

Consider each Twitch directory a tiny food court in which each channel is a restaurant you have the option to try, but until you eat their food you may not know whether it tastes good. Also in this food court, a visible ranking system displays how many people are eating at each restaurant at this very moment. Given you have no idea what any of these restaurants' food tastes like, it's tempting to assume the likelihood of one vendor's food being good increases with the number of people eating there. The difference is you don't have to wait to get your food on Twitch, so there isn't much of a downside to choosing the most popular stream. If there are too many choices, the average person will almost always go to where the most people are. If you've just opened a restaurant where nobody is eating yet, you may never even be considered as a choice.

Sound Advice from tehMorag (Twitch.tv/TehMorag)

Have the confidence to know you're not screwing up. Avoid letting yourself think, "Oh, I'm a failure, I'm not doing enough—I see this other caster doing really well." You might look at their chat real quick, and everyone's so happy. But then you go back to your five-hour broadcast, and that one person said you were terrible because you didn't answer them. At that point, avoid the trap of putting yourself down. It's impossible to answer everyone.

On the other hand, this might seem really cold, but blame yourself for everything. It's easy to point a finger at something you don't like, but if you blame yourself and you find a way to overcome it and conquer it, that's the best. If you point fingers at others or other things, it screams insecurity. It shows you aren't willing to go that extra mile. Smaller casters tend to feel they aren't being helped. There's a sense of entitlement that can grow from that. If you point your finger at Twitch, at the mods, at your viewers, at the life all around you that's giving you problems... there are ways around all of these "issues." Some things are out of your hands, but there's a way to overcome everything.

It comes down to how much effort you want to put into solving problems. If I have this problem, I'm going to solve it this way. If I still have this problem, what can I change to account for that? If it's going to happen all the time and I can't change it, then can I change something around it? And at the end of the day, you need to ask yourself if it's still worth it. Do you still want to endure the pain to push forward? You can't escape pain, but you can find ways to overcome it and push past it.

Highlight a problem, say it could be better, and then tell yourself what you're going to do about it. Tell yourself you're confident and that you're going to overcome it.

The biggest and most important element of a career is opportunity. A live broadcasting career is full of opportunities to do something with your passion. Every career has opportunities to grow, either as a person or as a professional, and life on Twitch is no different. It's hard to start a career, but it's incredibly hard to put down once you start having fun with it.

If you've read this far into the book, you may already understand a lot this. If you don't, this may answer your concerns about the growth of your channel and why it might feel stagnant. The point is, a career isn't something you do for money, although that's a key element to sustaining your career. To have a career on Twitch, you need the passion and dedication to think around obstacles and adjust to the situations that arise. Live and breathe the gaming industry, and use the tools you have (or that we gave you) to help you move forward. If you do anything less than that, you might be considered a hobbyist. Streaming as a hobby or streaming part-time is not a bad thing by any means, even if you make a little money in the process. However, if you wish to make a career out of streaming, you have to consider turning your part-time hobby into a full time passion.

Moving from Part-Time to Full-Time

Before we dive into what you should expect when you go full-time, we should discuss what becoming a full-time streamer means. Part-time streaming consists of roughly twenty-five hours of streaming or off-stream work per week. You might see successful streamers stream five hours a day, five days a week and still be considered full-time broadcasters. What you don't see is the additional twenty hours per week they spend working on their stream; answering emails; sitting in meetings; speaking with artists, managers, and agents; keeping up with social media posts; and making sure their hardware doesn't break down. The point is, anyone who streams twenty-five hours a week and has a respectably large audience has probably been doing it for a long time and knows how to make those twenty-five hours highly memorable and entertaining. It also probably means they've earned a lot of followers who know exactly when to expect to see that person online, so they don't have to build their live audience from scratch each day. This comes with being a full-time streamer and developing a career in online entertainment.

Full-time streamers spend about forty to fifty hours a week working, sometimes much more than that. Other times, the efficiency they've honed through experience enables them to finish a ton of work within those fifty hours. Between writing this book, maintaining a full-time streaming career, and spending a little time with my loved ones, I've spent eighty hours per week working on something.

They say, "Choose a job you love, and you will never have to work a day in your life." The truth is, even if you love your career, a job is still a job, and work is hard even if it's extremely rewarding.

Streaming full-time and turning it into a career is hard, it can be exhausting, and you cannot predict the future of your channel. At least in an office job, you can place odds on getting promoted a few times if you work there long enough. In a streaming career, you may never even become a Twitch partner, let alone make enough money to sustain a lifestyle, and it may not matter how talented you are. However, the more talent you have and the more knowledge you acquire to use your talent properly, the greater your chance for success; but again, it's still only a chance.

What to Expect Once You Make the Transition

If you ask a full-time broadcaster for advice about going full-time, the most common joke answer is, "don't do it." Then, when you ask again because you think they're joking, they might respond with, "no, really, don't do it." They remember the moment they made the same transition. The thing that often gets left behind in that answer is why they decided to make the transition in the first place. Streaming on Twitch is something you have to love. If you don't love streaming, there's absolutely no point in doing it. You shouldn't do it for the money because there isn't any money in it if you don't love doing it. You can't do it as a way to get paid to play video games all day—again, there's no money in Twitch if you don't love doing it. You definitely won't do it because it's easy. The failure rate is too high to make the transition to full-time streaming unless you know you're willing to give it your best shot. And if you fail, you can still say you tried to make it in one of the most volatile industries on the planet. In fact, you should expect to fail at some things. This isn't to say you can't make a real career out of livestreaming, but if you aren't failing at something every day, week, month, or year, then you aren't trying to make yourself better at it.

There's no need to reinvent the wheel; the wheel has already been created, molded, and mass produced because it sells extremely well. The biggest broadcasters out there aren't doing anything completely different from what you may have seen on television or even in Twitch's early days. However, it's their unique version of it. They've refined a successful formula to make it more attractive to an audience that knows what it likes.

Why Make the Transition?

There are many reasons to be afraid of taking the plunge to become a full-time streamer. Likewise, there are many reasons it can be the way to go if you really care about what you're doing.

Starting something by yourself takes way too much time. The amount of time you have to work on your stream and make sure everything's updated and relevant is far too high when you factor in how often you must stream to make any of it mean anything.

It's difficult to be taken seriously if you don't seem to take your channel seriously. People spend so much time watching streams on Twitch that, even as a full-timer, you won't be able to stream enough for most your audience to be satisfied with you alone. So, if you're a part of your followers' lives for only a small amount of time, it's very hard for them to invest in you.

Twitch is always—and I mean always—on. Twitch is a twenty-four seven, three hundred sixty-five day-a-year platform. At any point from the dawn of its existence to this very moment, someone is watching. If you wish to be relevant to the largest possible audience, you will always feel the need to stream more and more every day. Obviously, there's a limit to how much any human can do before it becomes very unhealthy, which is why I consider the term "full-time" to be interchangeable with the word "maximum." Full-time can mean many things to many different broadcasters, but I consider full-time to mean the maximum amount of time you can spend on your stream without going crazy, and still leaving some time for other activities. Maximums are different for everybody.

LIVESTREAMER INTERVIEW: The Hunter Wild (Twitch.tv/TheHunterWild)

Q: Any final advice for new or casual livestreamers who want to take their channel to the next level?

A: I'm a big attitude, concept, and approach kind of guy. I think one of the best pieces of advice I can give, which also seems universal, is to create a mission for your stream and a vision for where you want it to end up. I don't care how much research you have to do or how many websites and blog posts you need to visit to figure it out, but create something that only you can create. It will guide how you move through the continual evolution of your stream, your brand, your content, and how you get to shape that.

Without exception, every single broadcaster has to do this if they want livestreaming to be more than a hobby.

Act III: In for the Long Haul

Welcome to Act III

First, congratulations on making it this far in your career. If you are at a point where Act III is relevant to you, then you should know that you've accomplished more than the vast majority of broadcasters on Twitch. Some might not understand what it takes to get to the point at which you are making a living, running your own business, saving money, and investing that money. Although this chapter doesn't provide specific business advice, we hope the advice that we do provide helps you generate revenue via your influence, and keeps your business safe while doing so.

Act III is for those who have experience streaming on Twitch and have grown their channel to a point where you, for example, may not have enough time to respond to emails and other inquiries that you're getting on a regular basis. This section also covers contracts, partnerships, and sponsors. It details things to look out for in relation to these topics, and how to protect yourself in the process. Although it may sound simple when you are focused on maintaining your audience and making sure that your content is at the highest quality, you should read the information in Act III to help you quickly find red flags and ensure that you're getting the best deal for your work.

Broadcasters are entertainers, IT support specialists, public relations representatives, and pretty much anything that involves running a business. As the business of livestreaming gets larger, services will become more accessible and affordable, however, for now the feeling amongst broadcasters is that they must do everything themselves. If a broadcaster needs help, there are a lot of people who will be willing to help, but broadcasters don't often understand that some people will help them without asking for anything in return. It's important to remember that you likely didn't get to this position by yourself and you probably helped a lot of people along the way, too. Keep this in mind and you will always have the support you need.

If you're an artist of any sort, then you are also part of a tight-knit, expanding art industry that is also growing closer as its members support its peers. This is relevant for a few reasons because it means most everyone is accessible, as they know exactly where you're coming from most of the time. More importantly, if you act unprofessionally in an industry where your professional skill is being scrutinized, then that news will spread to others in the industry. This doesn't happen for malicious reasons. Instead, it's the fact that this industry was built to look after one other. So if someone in the industry gets wronged by another person, the affected person doesn't want something similar to happen to anyone else. That person may send out warnings to others close to them. Normally, if the person doing something wrong isn't just doing this to one person, but it more than likely treating others with disrespect. So be polite, be professional, and when someone thinks there is a misunderstanding, hear them out and listen, because someone's word can go a long way in the gaming industry.

Before we dive into Act III, it is important to know a lot of the topics that are covered are not required of each broadcaster. The content in this chapter may be more relevant to some than others, so read it in its entirety and take all the advice to heart. The sections in this chapter cover things like management and moving beyond Twitch. If you haven't built your channel to a level at which you need management, or you're just not influential enough to receive offers, these topics may not be relevant. If you're truly curious about what it means to be at this level—or what it feels like once you get there—then this chapter will be a good read. On the other hand, this chapter will definitely appeal to those who have reached a higher level of success, so a thorough read of this chapter is a must. Without further ado, let's get into the complicated stuff.

Words of Wisdom—wgrates

Q: Any final advice for new or casual livestreamers who want to take their channel to the next level?

A: Have fun and be respectful the entire time. Just because you're online and you may not use your real name, that doesn't make anything you say or do less important. The way you interact with people should be the same way you interact with people on the street or in another broadcaster's channel. Be classy. People respond well to that.

Contracts, Partners, and Sponsors

Scary? Maybe, But Don't Be Afraid

One component of your career growth as a broadcaster and influencer of opinions is that others want to help you profit from your popularity—in turn, it helps them profit from your popularity. Before we discuss your relationships with professionals who wish to do business with you, it's important to understand a few things about your position. That position can be one of great stress, responsibility for your image and business, and a constant need to innovate, but most importantly it's a position of great power. You make the call regarding whether to expose your community to a product, game, brand, or anything a company might offer you. We really do mean anything, because people always look for ways to sell something to consumers. We don't wish to imply that such companies are evil in any way. However, there's always a purpose to a sponsorship and, if it's a good one, then both parties benefit.

Between subscriptions, tips, and cheering via Bits in your channel, there are plenty of opportunities to earn a decent paycheck. However, to achieve this, your community must support you each and every month. This creates a lot of pressure for you to put on a great show every day to keep your viewers interested. Your audience's interest is important anyway, but when people invest money every month, they often watch with a critical eye. Most people don't mean to be judgmental when they spend money on your channel. Rather, it's sort of natural for them to feel invested because they literally are, even if it isn't by much.

LIVESTREAMER INTERVIEW: Sir Slaw (Twitch.tv/SirSlaw)

Q: Twitch as a hobby vs. a profession: How would you advise someone who's setting goals for himself or herself?

A: Livestreaming is hard. There's a ridiculously high failure rate, and most streamers quit livestreaming after their first three months. We need to be honest with ourselves first and foremost. People need to understand that it's safer and makes more sense for this to start out as a hobby. For those who have loftier goals and turn this into a career with Twitch partnership and full-time streaming, start with baby steps. Start small; try to get one person to return to your next stream. Then two. Then three, four, five people. Also, a great way to grow your channel is to play a game at the beginning or end of the directory.

First Things First

Even if it seems trivial, creating a business email account and adding it to all your public profiles is one of the most important things you can do. You can place your normal email account on your profiles if you like, but you'll find it much easier to keep things organized if you have a separate account. If you're moving into the Act III phase, then you're interested in monetizing your broadcasts beyond having your community fund the stream. However, you can't monetize beyond subscriptions and other first-party means unless companies that want to work with you know how to contact you quickly and easily.

It's also important to know your value. You may not know have a precise figure, but that's okay because it's difficult to calculate. Besides, your value fluctuates throughout your time in the industry. You'll want to familiarize yourself with a whole mess of information, and we'll get to that. In the meantime, take care of your email and make it available to the people who need it. Moreover, adopt the mentality that you have a value, and begin to consider what it might be. You're definitely in pole position when you start to deal with companies from a business perspective.

Broadcasting Value

Every Twitch broadcast has a value. Each broadcast, whether it's a game, a piece of art, or a production of any kind, shows something to the world for a reason. That reason could be one of many things, but the inspiration and effort behind the broadcast has meaning and value. Whether you think the game you're playing is good or bad, there are always people out there who care about it and how it's perceived. If you show your audience what you think is good and bad about a game, people will care about your opinion; it will hold value as a criticism. This is why you, as a media creator, are so important to the consumer entertainment ecosystem.

The real challenge is not to understand that your content on Twitch has value, but to determine your content's numerical value to those who have an interest in your influence. Your community finds value in your entertainment, and they show their appreciation in many ways, but for this conversation, we're interested in monetary consideration. A company that sells a product or an idea can show its appreciation for your value by sharing its advertising budget with you in return for your support, whatever form your support may take. You can find a few soft numbers indicating how you should be compensated, as calculated by several highly trusted sources. In the current broadcasting climate, value cost to a sponsor is normally calculated per viewer per minute at anywhere from $.011-.03. The Online Performers Group, a group that manages some of the top broadcasters in the industry, has used these figures for several years.

As always in this business, many factors go into calculating an exact cost when you negotiate rates with a sponsor. If you use our figures as a starting point and expand from there, you should be able to strike a deal that's good for both you and the sponsor, thus developing a real relationship.

What Makes a Partnership?

The word partnership gets thrown around a lot in the online entertainment industry. As a Twitch

broadcaster, you may be offered many types of partnerships. In its purest form, a partnership is a relationship between two parties in which they can directly support each other in an equitable way. We mention the term equitable for a reason. Many programs being marketed to broadcasters give them a cut of the profits they generate, normally a small amount, and ask them to provide all of the promotion without much support; we call this an affiliation. These two terms, affiliate and partner, are very well explained by the Twitch Partnership and Affiliate programs—they are often treated similarly. Partnerships are meant to keep the broadcaster involved in as many ways as possible to help grow a product's community. It can be hard to understand a program's feel and the way it affects you personally and professionally as a broadcaster. Pure numbers and revenue shares between the parties can sometimes explain it, but numbers vary so much between programs that they aren't a consistent guideline.

The Warframe Partner Program is currently one of the most impressive partner programs. *Warframe* is a free-to-play action game with a large multiplayer co-op community focused on completing missions around a fictionally enhanced future version of our solar system. There's a lot to do in the game, and there are many ways to involve members of your community whilst playing the game. Digital Extremes, the company behind *Warframe*, enlists broadcasters who are truly in love with the game, providing them with information and community support for their viewers. The company is highly involved with its broadcasters, and this connection gives partners plenty of opportunities for giveaways to help retain subscribers, as well as paid opportunities at live events and online announcements. There is no direct revenue share, so there is no added pressure to sell a product—instead, enjoy the game with the community. There are many great partnership programs out there, but it's important to know what makes a partnership or an affiliation. If the partner you hope to work with isn't a game company, make sure your contacts are willing to stay engaged with you and offer creative ways to help you make your channel better with their product, rather than simply profit from you.

Before You Sign the Contract

Read it! Actually read the actual words in the actual document. There's no such thing as a normal contract, and you should be especially concerned if the person who wants you to sign tells you that it's "just a normal contract." Every contract, especially one sent to many people within a short amount of time, is written to favor one party's interests. In most situations, contracts are written to be as fair as possible, but bias always arises and sometimes clouds objective fairness. It's up to you to read and be sure that terms are balanced and fair for you. It's important to remember that absolutely everything is negotiable in business.

You've probably seen huge signs hanging in electronic stores exclaiming they will match online prices. This strategy is designed to ensure you purchase the products you need from their store. You initiate a negotiation with the store by shopping there. Initially, you can either pay a premium and pick up your brand new monitor right then and there, or you can save some money and take your business elsewhere. The store doesn't want you to leave without buying, so reminding you that you can negotiate helps ensure they keep your business. Obviously, stores have policies to keep you from convincing store associates to give you a price even lower than the matching counterpart. But have you ever tried negotiating with a store manager or, more effectively, the store owner? Businesses want to stay in business, and in order to keep your patronage, they are, more often than not, willing to work with you to make sure that happens. This doesn't always work, but you never know until you try. There's no rule that says negotiating isn't allowed. Making deals as a broadcaster is no different.

If a company wants to work with you, then its representatives have decided they need you to help grow their business. It's their job to partner with people like you. Just remember, it's also their job to protect the company's profit margin. This doesn't mean every company tries to make you do a ton of work for them while giving you rock-bottom compensation. However, some do, and they really think they can get away with it because others have signed their contracts. On the other hand, sometimes they're simply unfamiliar with a broadcaster's role, and they don't realize exactly how much work they're asking of you before you actually inform them.

Reading and, more importantly, comprehending a contract is not necessarily the easiest thing to do. When you hear about a deal gone sour or one that started out bad and stayed that way, it's easy to assume the person who was wronged just didn't read the contract—they messed up by being lazy. Often, the truth is that the person signing off on the deal did read the contract, but something was hidden in legalese or terms only business professionals would understand.

A company that really cares about its relationship with you and making sure you're comfortable will try to ensure you completely understand the terms of your agreement. Companies don't always intend to be confusing, but you should know it's always okay to ask questions, regardless of the circumstances. You should never be made to feel you can't ask questions—that's a red flag. Protect yourself against possible financial, social, and professional harm by making sure you're one hundred percent clear on your legal obligations. Don't be afraid to have other professionals, such as a lawyer or two, look at your agreement to be sure you're protected. Lawyers often cost some money, but unless they do some negotiating for you, the cost shouldn't be much, and it's well worth your effort to make sure you're safe.

Sponsorships Are Part of Your Brand

Your brand encompasses many aspects of your career. Some may say your brand is an amalgamation of everything you say and do. The things you endorse are no exceptions to this. You may have nothing to do with the production, manufacture, branding, or even who represents a product. However, the moment you endorse it, you connect yourself with that brand. If a partner company does something shady or immoral, it doesn't necessarily mean your brand will suffer a fatal blow, especially if you had no way of knowing something like that could ever happen. However, because you tied your brand to theirs, it's important to make a statement declaring you never knew about the problems that occurred until they were made public, and you did your research to ensure you signed up with a company you thought was trustworthy. This is simply to protect your brand, not to disparage your partner. Even if others make statements about the company or brand in question, those may also be untrue, and you could burn a bridge for no reason if you make disparaging remarks.

LIVESTREAMER INTERVIEW: TehMorag (Twitch.tv/TehMorag)

Q: At what point did you first start to think about branding for your channel?

A: Ten years ago! It's something I started thinking about before Twitch, just with me being online. It was a forum banner. It was my online username. It still puzzles me that people cycle their usernames online. Regardless of your brand, think of it this way: it's the act of erasing your existence in an online culture that's ever changing.

When I was first introduced to going online, I was in elementary school. I wanted to look up the full map of a game I was playing, so I sat at a library computer as it chugged away to display the full map. Even then, I had an older username that I got rid of because I found it wasn't a smart way to have a username. I ended up choosing another name, a name from a book that was cool, and it fit me. I used it online everywhere, and wherever you found me online you'd see the same username.

In a situation where a brand is revealed to be untrustworthy, the best thing you can do, as both a partner and the sponsored party, is to verify any accurate information and be as honest as you can be with your audience. What you say about a brand after an incident is completely up to you, but simply stating your position and how you feel about the situation is the best way to keep the trust between you and your community. Trust is important between people when there's money involved; your community trusts you to promote products they will like, even if some don't. Likewise, sponsors trust you to be honest with them, and I assume you expect the same of them. Do your research on a company before you accept a sponsorship, so your trust can go a lot farther in any professional relationship you may establish.

Disclosure and Honesty

In the United States, there's a branch of government called the Federal Trade Commission, or the FTC for short. Its job is to protect consumers. As one of the biggest industries in the world, video game entertainment involves a great deal of money, and that occasionally draws shady individuals. As the livestreaming industry grows, there will be individuals and companies that either don't know what they're doing or don't want to play by the rules. Many folks believe they must sometimes break rules to get things done. But the FTC enacts rules to protect consumers from being scammed, lied to, falsely advertised to, and so on. We advise you to visit *www.ftc.gov* and look through the website's Tips & Advice section to see recommendations regarding any streams you are paid to do. You should also search for articles like "The FTC's Endorsement Guides," and search for terms like #Ad or #Sponsored. You might get some results that make you think you've broken the law during some of your streams. Because you're reading this now, you'll at least know there are ways to protect yourself against crimes that break consumer law.

One major rule is that, if you are paid to do something, whether it's to play a game, tweet about a game or product, or even talk about something for thirty seconds, you should at the very least disclose that you're being paid by a company to do those things. Regarding promotional content for which you directly receive money, the FTC normally requires you to include #Ad or #Sponsored in the forefront of your stream title, going-live tweet, or anywhere you tell your audience what you're doing. The point of this is to clearly, without a doubt, let your audience know you're being paid. You don't have to disclose how much you're being paid. In fact, doing so is usually a bad idea because you don't want it distract from your content. Nevertheless, you do have to disclose that the payment exists.

Why?

"Why do I have to publicly disclose that I'm being paid to play this game?" I receive this question a lot. Most people understand that transparency is the best way to earn your community's trust. But, in a few ways, that's not why you have to disclose this information. That explanation is accurate to the point that trust is the major reason for disclosure. Without proper disclosure, trust can be used as a weapon rather than a tool. If disclosure rules didn't exist, some broadcasters might take deals in which they're paid way too much money to play a game they truly don't like. But, instead of telling the truth, the deal might dictate they must say they love the game and make sure their audience believes them. Depending on their situation, some broadcasters might have a hard time saying no to such opportunities. FTC rules make it illegal for someone to do this.

There's a point at which one might say, although it's not okay to conceal when you're being paid to do something, nothing prohibits you from being dishonest about your opinion of a product. Ethically speaking, you shouldn't deceive viewers about your opinions of products, but nothing prohibits you from doing so, which is probably why the FTC developed its guidelines. I think you get it, but what I'm trying to say is, tell the truth or don't say anything at all.

Professional Truth vs. Unprofessional Conduct

There's a major difference between being truthful and just being rude. Some people don't quite understand the difference, but there is one. Obviously, when something's good and you enjoy it, it's easy to speak positively about the product. However, when you don't like something as much, it's important to be honest but fair. That being said, you should never take a sponsorship from something you either know or anticipate you won't like. But sometimes, despite playing part of a game or briefly trying a product, doing your research, and trusting what people tell you about it, you simply find something major that you don't like. It happens from time to time. The best practice in this situation is to talk about why you don't like it, or how it could be better. It may be helpful to make your audience aware of the faults you've identified, and then talk about the things you like, as well as the reasons you decided to take the sponsorship in the first place. Both the sponsor and your audience will appreciate genuine content. A sponsor will never enjoy seeing someone they hire tear apart a product they worked hard to create. Even if they aren't overjoyed that your review is less than glowing, as long as your review is tactful and fair, they should respect your judgment and know that your audience will value your opinion when they hire you again. And if their next product is a good one, your approval will sell even more copies than it would have if you had lied the first time around.

Stream Management

What Is Management?

Many of you have probably heard of community managers, or people who are paying attention to your stream, chat in your channel, interact with things that occur during your stream, and are generally fans of your channel. Essentially, community managers don't always know the business side of things as it relates to contracts, partnerships, sponsorships, etc. Typically, a community manager in a streamer's community is a volunteer who helps run the community. I have a community manager who goes by the name of NeonTiger, and a lead moderator who goes by the name of Gamertech; they both volunteered to work with the community. I probably wouldn't be where I am today without them. In fact, I bounce ideas off NeonTiger because he has a good amount of knowledge about what it takes to create successful content, and he also understands what my community likes. Gamertech focuses on making sure every moderator knows the rules and helps keep the bad things out of chat. In effect, he keeps everyone in line.

 We talk about community management and moderation in order to talk about stream management. There have been many cases in which community managers have become stream managers and broadcasters have learned how to manage other broadcasters' careers. Take HBFox for example; he is a natural moderator who became a highly valued member of TheHunterWild's channel. Eventually, companies started reaching out to TheHunterWild but he didn't have the extra time to handle all the inquiries. HBFox stepped in to take some of this responsibility and now runs some things like branding, negotiating deals with sponsors, all while keeping TheHunterWild's best interests in mind. HBFox was a community member, turned friend, turned valued moderator, turned manager, all in the span of several years. Essentially, a streamer must trust that whoever he or she chooses must have the streamer's best interests in mind.

You should know that HBFox and TheHunterWild were friends of Omeed Dariani, Jenn Dariani, and myself before any of us became professionally involved with each other, however that does not necessarily mean you should hire your friends to manage your career. HBFox happened to be really good at managing TheHunterWild's stream and he would probably be really good at managing anyone's stream because of his talent and skill set. Omeed and Jenn own and operate one of, if not the best management company on Twitch known as the Online Performers Group. These are professionals who know how to do their job, but most importantly these are people who broadcasters trust to manage their careers. If you choose a friend to help in this regard—or a professional with high integrity—select someone who will look after your career and future. Take some time and choose wisely, because there's absolutely no rush to hire someone who will be no good for your career.

What Does a Manager Do?

Basically, a manager can help lighten a streamer's workload. One misconception is that a manager will get you work and make sure you're making money. Well, part of that is true. They're not out on the streets offering your services to companies. That is what an agent does in this business. A manager will ensure that you are always making money by keeping your brand intact and keeping you away from bad deals. A manager is there to help when companies are seeking an endorsement, but you have no time to research information about them. Or, as Omeed said to me when we sat down to talk about this book: "I try my best to solve clients' problems."

In order to solve problems, a manager needs to know who you are. For example, if you're feeling unsafe on a job that your manager found for you, it probably means that your manager made a bad deal.

Managers make their business thrive by ensuring your business is thriving. Although managers take different cuts of your profits, a good manager will also make sure you are being paid fairly for your work. A good manager should also know when to turn down a deal that doesn't fit your brand or simply isn't a good deal. This is another case in which trust is the key to everything. If you do not have a strong relationship with your manager, then you probably aren't in a great situation.

Strengths in Management

Managers come in all shapes and sizes. Some manage the top talent in your field, while others manage talent who are still learning the ropes. Some managers are experienced and some are brand new to the game. Here are some strengths to look for in a potential manager.

- **She or he listens to you.** Communication is one of the most important things for a manager. A manager must listen to their client and use that information to help them.

- **The ability to say no.** "No" shouldn't be the only word that your manager knows, but it should be in their vocabulary especially if you plan on letting him or her negotiate deals. You don't want a manager who says yes to every offer or deal that comes along just because it has dollar signs in front of it.

- **Resourcefulness.** Managers can't solve every problem if they don't have, or know how to use, any resources available to them. Whether that means getting you out of a sketchy deal, getting a hotel room at the last minute, etc. No matter the case, if it has something to do with your professional life, a manager should be able to find time to meet all your needs.

- **Allow you to be the boss.** A manager works for you, but you must listen to the people trying to help you in order for them to do their best. A good manager should represent you well, while making sure it is something that you would want them to do. Basically, this means that if you need something, they are going to do what they can to get it done.

In the end, a manager is there to help you manage your life.

Final Thoughts

Final thoughts about management with Omeed Dariani, CEO of Online Performers Group

The first thing is to understand that what you do is new. It's a new medium, it's a new art form, but there are other art forms that have come before; there is other talent who have come before. So, there's no reason to re-invent the wheel. Look at what has happened in other industries, how talent has worked, what other deals have worked, and what has made them successful, and look at that more than anything else. The biggest thing I see is that everyone wants to rush. It's a slow process. Becoming an actor is not something you do in two years; it takes a lifetime. People tend to think, "I've been streaming for two years, I've been streaming for three years. I should be very successful." The reality is that to become a successful talent is difficult and it's time consuming because you have to get good at it. Not everyone can succeed at this. I think there's a misconception that anyone can stream because, technically, anyone can. Anyone can buy a computer, turn it on, and play a game. Anyone can memorize the lines and stand on stage in a play, but that does not mean anyone can be successful. That's kind of a hard fact of life to learn. So, if you want to do this and if you're passionate about it, you will have to focus and dedicate your life to it, the same way a musician has dedicated their life to music and an actor has dedicated their life to their art. If you're not willing to do that, you're not going to succeed. So, people tend to rush toward, "I need a manager, I need an agent, I need to start doing deals," when the reality is, if you become good at what you do, all of that will come in good time.

The people who are the most successful actors are found in acting workshops, or in voice audition workshops, or that kind of thing. The secret is that everyone who cares about talent are the people who are paying attention to up and coming people. If you are good, then people are going to see that. So, focus on what you're good at, become an expert at that, become the best person at what you do, and the rest will come. You will notice that in your community already. People will volunteer to be mods, they'll volunteer to do art for your channel, they'll volunteer to promote your channel. People will come out of the woodwork when you're good at what you do. We notice streamers years before they become big. The data shows us, other streamers refer you, so become good at what you do, first, and the rest of it will come naturally.

Opportunities to Fit Your Brand

Brand Solidity

There's a lot of talk about brands in this book, as the concept is extremely important and fits into many conversations about livestreaming on Twitch. Your brand shapes the world around your channel; it tells people how to think about you and your stream. If you still have trouble understanding what your brand might be, or how it may have developed up to this point, then finding the right opportunities to fit your brand will be difficult and possibly damaging to your brand.

If you know where your brand is and where it's going, start thinking about how to expand your opportunities. Too many people try to rush to opportunities; understand, just because someone else takes an opportunity doesn't mean you lose out on it. In some situations, competition might be part of the equation, but for the most part competition matters only when specific variables line up for the same opportunity. Most companies want to expand their brand to as many places as possible. And with this industry's growth, there simply aren't enough broadcasters to fulfill current needs. Some opportunities are completely wrong for certain broadcasters but they take them anyway and set themselves back.

Most people are aware of what's right for them. But sometimes getting a certain dollar amount to stream a game feels like the perfect opportunity because you're getting paid to do something you love. It may be a great ego boost when a company offers to pay you to play a game for an hour. Keep in mind, however, that many offers require you to reach certain goals to receive the full payment. If you're a Twitch partner, you may have seen this specific situation in a first-party feature called the Bounty Board.

We won't go into too much detail about bounties and how the Bounty Board works, because the program may change by the time you read this. However, the Bounty Board is a great tool to see if your brand has synergy with the games that this program offers. You may find a game featuring the Queen Gungeon Ant in which you destroy bosses in seconds, or you end up getting a block of wood with zero damage upgrades. (That's for any *Enter the Gungeon* fans out there.) In plain English, you may find something on the Bounty Board that works for your brand and audience, allowing you to get paid the full bounty—note that you won't be paid more for exceeding your goal. On the other hand, you may find something that seems appealing, but it doesn't work for your audience and nobody shows up. Or, you may just have a bad day—the time you choose to do a bounty ends up being a slow period, which completely wastes the opportunity. The point is, this game we call the Twitch Meta is never easy to predict. There's no magic formula to make every day perfect. But the stronger your brand and the more you know about how it influences people, the better you'll be at finding the right opportunities to fit it, which gives you the best chance at a successful stream.

Merchandise Is a Great Appetizer

Everybody likes stuff. This is an easy call. They especially like stuff when it's branded with their favorite broadcasters' logos, emotes, memes, mascots, community—whatever—as long as it has some tie to the person they like to watch. T-shirts are the most popular items Twitch broadcasters sell, but people are finding more and more ways to get their faces or logos on physical items across a wide spectrum. As I look around my office, I can see hundreds of items I've purchased, been given, and had made for myself. Branded merchandise offers a personal connection, and when you mix that with fandom, items become a lot more valuable to the folks buying them.

Merchandise is a great starter opportunity for broadcasters of any size. Hiring an artist to create your merchandise design can be expensive, but for the most part that's the only expense when you use companies that print per purchase. So, if you're okay investing some money in a design, you can print shirts, coffee mugs, stickers, sweatshirts, underwear, mouse pads—the list just goes on and on.

A Peek Into the "Musk" with TheHunterWild

Q: How does "Musk" fit in with your brand?

 A: Now, that's an interesting question. Presumably musk is a good scent. I've learned over time that a lot of people don't think it's meant to be good. That if you have this musky smell, it's like, "Ew, you nasty," and you haven't showered in, like, a month. But it's supposed to be a sort of attractive and appealing scent. It's very natural and the scent goes away if you bathe a lot. I like the natural, being a little wild, being more biologically anchored. And it only matters to other people, how they perceive you. Scent is one of the senses people can use to experience other people, and it's a powerful one. Scent memory is one of the big anchors we have to our remembered experiences.

Q: How has your branding changed throughout your livestream career? What caused the branding changes or updates?

A: It hasn't changed dramatically. Consistency is very important in a brand, but at the same time I'd never advise someone to be afraid of changing their brand to the point that they'd never do it. Sometimes, you reach a critical point where it needs to change, and you have a vision that doesn't include what you currently have. It's okay to rebrand when you need something fresh and new.

At the same time, I've seen a pretty rampant rebranding trend where people, if they're dissatisfied with their stream, will just rebrand hoping it's the thing that solves it. But you almost always have other critical concerns in that case. But yeah, consistency is very important, yet I'd never be afraid of changing if you need to.

Live Events

Convention Streams

Another common opportunity for broadcasters is the offer to stream from a booth at a convention. It's attractive because broadcasting consistency is one of a streamer's most important traits. So, when you're out of the office and you simply can't stream, it can hamper your channel's growth. Taking a paid opportunity to stream from a company's booth doesn't always occur to a broadcaster. Remember, everything is negotiable, which means when you see a tweet or message about a company that needs to fill streaming slots for their booth, your broadcast benefits their brand as well. There isn't much of a difference between streaming someone's game from their convention booth and receiving a key to stream it from your own home for free.

Companies can get talent to stream their games because broadcasters get an opportunity to do something they otherwise don't get to do. However, there's one catch: you almost never land a promoted stream during the convention itself or even within the same week because agreements have to be drafted, reviewed, approved, and signed by all stakeholders, which can take a lot of time. Considering that you shouldn't do anything without an official agreement, broadcasters looking to take sponsored opportunities should plan ahead and try not to take too many spur-of-the-moment gigs.

Live Appearances and Hosting Events

Hosting gigs and live appearances are less common opportunities, but they can be extremely valuable and fun, yet sometimes very risky. They can be valuable for the company contacts and fruitful business relationships you may foster. If you're good at hosting and presenting, sometimes in front of a live audience, then gigs like this can really snowball. Some of the greatest moments I've had in front of an audience were when I could show off at a cool esports event or just talk about products I already respected.

As we know, in broadcasting or entertainment gigs, the more fun you have, the better the show is. So, if live events are fun for you, there's a good chance they could be a great avenue for you to explore. The risk lies in events that simply aren't produced in a professional manner. Most productions are extremely difficult to mess up, which makes the risk fairly low, but it still exists. This is a big reason why it's important to make sure your contract is sound, and you make sure you're protected in the event you have to bail from the event when things just don't smell right ... sometimes literally.

Photo Shoots

As a broadcaster who uses a camera, you may assume a group of people enjoys looking at you. At the very least, they enjoy your content enough to tolerate seeing you onscreen, and that means they will likely enjoy photo shoots with you as a subject. As fitness and modeling becomes more and more popular on Twitch, so do the sponsors that need models for their products. Companies that sell wearable products typically hire professional models to show off their wares. However, as the world of wearables evolves, so does the audience. Twitch viewers are becoming more and more attached to their favorite broadcasters because, unlike Hollywood actors, they are much more approachable and accessible, given folks can interact with them every time they're onscreen. This, by itself, makes their images much more powerful per viewer than anonymous models when it comes to selling products. So, the more your community feels attached to you, the better your chances of getting a photo shoot or modeling gig.

Creativity and Miscellaneous Projects

Up to this point, we've discussed opportunities proven to work for Twitch broadcasters. Our list is by no means exhaustive. We encourage you to be experimental. Use your creativity and drive to try new things. Start writing down ideas and figure out how to pitch them. If a company likes your pitch, there's a good chance they'll work with you to ensure they get a good result.

I've always wanted to try comedic skits promoting brands and products on Twitch. We see this in traditional commercials all the time, but it can be risky. A mediocre skit or poor execution quickly falls flat, but using humor as a promotional tool can be very successful. A comedic skit around a product could really make a powerful ad, especially when your audience sees you delivering the endorsement. If you can figure out how to do this well, live on stream, please let me know.

Thinking Outside the Platform

Before We Leave You ...

Before we leave you with lots to think about, and likely many questions we simply couldn't answer in one book, we'd like to provide some parting words. First, consider Twitch as a stepping stone for your entire entertainment career. Twitch and live broadcasting has a lot of potential and, frankly, it's still quite young. The better you get at being a talented gamer, actor, singer, artist, or whatever you do, the more opportunities will open up for you to use those skills beyond Twitch. Rise to your greatest potential. Keep your eyes open and make friends with the world, because humanity is your enemy only when you choose it to be. You will be attacked and you will need to defend yourself, but if you aren't an instigator, you can embody the change you seek for a world that may sometimes get you down. To quote the greatest hip-hop artist in the world, "Peace, love, and positivity. Regardless of race, religion, color, creed, or sexual orientation." Remember to stay positive, play more video games, and read more comics. Now, I leave you with some parting words from our friends.

Parting Words from Our Friends

Absolutely use whoever you're watching on Twitch as a guiding light. You can't lose sight of yourself, so don't try to be them. Take what you think is valuable from them and put your own spin on it. Be your own person, and emulate the things you want to see in the world. Try not to put on a facade—it's hard, we all sort of put on facades throughout our days as we interact with people. But it's pervasive and it's a little toxic, and it bleeds into other parts of our lives, and suddenly it's unstoppable. And then the person you put on stream isn't the person you really are. And, god forbid, you blow up as the person you're not—there's no telling what could happen from there.

- SirSlaw

Try to find a few things that are you, and truly you, and try to share that with the world. Everybody has that weird uncle, or that awkward friend, or the cool kid that they grew up with. These people stick out in their minds, and that's for a reason: the inflections, the mannerisms that make them unique. Find what your mannerisms are, what makes you, you, and be proud to share them with the world.

- Venalis

I'm a big attitude, concept, and approach kind of guy. I think one of the best pieces of advice I can give, which also seems universal, is to create a mission for your stream and a vision for where you want it to end up. I don't care how much research you have to do or how many websites and blog posts you need to visit to figure it out, but create something that only you can create. It will guide how you move through the continual evolution of your stream, your brand, your content, and how you get to shape that.

Without exception, every single broadcaster has to do this if they want livestreaming to be more than a hobby.

- TheHunterWild

Have fun and be respectful the entire time. Just because it's online and you may not be using your real name, that doesn't make anything you say or do less important. The way you interact with people on stream should be the same way you interact with people on the street, or in another broadcaster's channel. Be classy; people respond well to that.

- wgrates

Have the confidence to know you aren't screwing up. Avoid letting yourself think, "Oh, I'm a failure, I'm not doing enough—I see this other caster doing really well." You might look at their chat real quick, and everyone's so happy. But then you go back to your five-hour broadcast, and that one person said you were terrible because you didn't answer them. At that point, avoid the trap of putting yourself down. It's impossible to answer everyone.

On the other hand, this might seem really cold, but blame yourself for everything. It's easy to point a finger at something you don't like, but if you blame yourself and you find a way to overcome it and conquer it, that's the best. If you point fingers at others or other things, it screams insecurity. It shows you aren't willing to go that extra mile. Smaller casters tend to feel they aren't being helped. There's a sense of entitlement that can grow from that. If you point your finger at Twitch, at the mods, at your viewers, at the life all around you that's giving you problems ... there are ways around all of these "issues." Some things are out of your hands, but there's a way to overcome everything.

It comes down to how much effort you want to put into solving problems. If I have this problem, I'm going to solve it this way. If I still have this problem, what can I change to account for that? If it's going to happen all the time and I can't change it, then can I change something around it? And at the end of the day, you need to ask yourself if it's still worth it. Do you still want to endure the pain to push forward? You can't escape pain, but you can find ways to overcome it and push past it.

Highlight a problem, say it could be better, and then tell yourself what you're going to do about it. Tell yourself you're confident and that you're going to overcome it.

- tehMorag

The fact that you're already reading this and dedicating time to learning about streaming is putting you far ahead of most new streamers. A lot of people just expect they can hit the Start Streaming button and success with flow their way, but the reality is it takes a lot of time, commitment, and understanding of streaming to create success. Set realistic goals and evaluate your own stream regularly!

– Lowco

It's easy to feel discouraged as a streamer, because you kind of feel like you're working by yourself, for yourself. Getting some energy from your community is really important. When I can't stream, I let my community know, and they're receptive to that and encourage me. Get close to your community in ways that let you know what you're doing right and wrong, and just be there for them. Even if you have only five people watching you, you matter for those five people. So, keep that in mind.

– missharvey

The streaming grind may look like "just playing video games," but it is a lot harder and more taxing than it looks. A lot of work, a lot of late nights, and a lot of long streams go into building your channel. But if it's something you're passionate about and you're willing to make changes that will help you grow, you'll be just fine.

– LittleSiha

Twitch Terms of Service

 This publication is designed to provide accurate and authoritative information in regard to the subject matter covered. It is sold with the understanding that the publisher is not engaged in rendering legal, accounting, or other professional services. If you require legal advice or other expert assistance, you should seek the services of a competent professional.

What are Terms of Service?

Let's start with the basics. Many channels are suspended or even banned each month because their owners fail to follow the rules stated within the Terms of Service, or TOS, as they are known to many Twitch users. Terms of service are stated in every online platform used by other humans (e.g., online multiplayer games, image uploading platforms, online chat programs, etc.). It makes sense that the average person doesn't take the time to read through the terms of service for everything they use because there simply isn't enough time to read all of them. However, you care about what it means to be a performer on the Twitch platform, and how the company interprets your content matters with regard to the TOS rules.

The best way to think about any terms of service is to understand they exist to protect the entity that wrote them. This doesn't mean they want to censor users and keep them from doing anything on their platform. They want to keep their users happy and using their platform as much as possible. A set of rules is essential, and knowing them is important to protect both yourself and your brand. This chapter will help you understand at least how to read the TOS in a way that makes sense for you as a broadcaster.

 Disclaimer: Like anything in this industry, including this book, the future is unpredictable, which means the Terms of Service on Twitch will change many times from here. However, this book was written in a way that we hope will help you for the rest of your career.

Privacy

The protection of your privacy is an important piece of any Terms of Service document. In an industry where many users frequently give out information that may or may not be sensitive, a privacy section is always essential. Because the Twitch platform provides the type of services it does, there are many opportunities for privacy to be breached. Privacy breaches are extremely bad for any brand, including channel owners', so it makes sense that the privacy section is so big that it has its own document.

The Privacy Policy will change just as often as the Terms of Service. As a broadcaster, familiarize yourself with the Privacy Policy, as it directly affects you every time you stream, subscribe, follow, and so forth. More importantly, it will help you run your channel in a way that keeps your viewers' privacy intact.

The reason you, as someone who creates content on Twitch, are responsible is that, although Twitch takes responsibility for writing a Privacy Policy and Terms of Service, you may be tempted to use a third-party service or software that gathers some type of data from your viewers. This isn't to say you have to avoid third-party tools, but you may be more diligent about researching how these tools handle policies like this.

It's important to remember that information is good for many things. However, like most online interactions, there's definitely a line that's easy to cross, so attention to detail and how you may handle your channel can be very particular. Generally, when it comes to understanding an audience, you want certain demographic information, such as age range, gender, and geographic location. These details don't seem to bother people too often, but there's a reason laws exist to prevent acquiring certain information. Twitch doesn't gather a lot of this information, which is why we bring up this topic in the first place. It's easier to keep users' information safe if said information is never acquired. However, some entities attempt to gather this information because of its value. Beware of tools that may attempt to do this when you use them on your stream. Remember that what you use directly affects how you appear to other brands, but more importantly to your viewers and peers.

License and User Content

A license is something an entity that owns a copyright, trademark, or any intellectual property may grant to another entity. For example, whoever runs a channel on a platform may be granted the right to use another entity's property within the limitations listed in the license. That's a very basic description of what it means to have and use a license. But there's much more to understand before you jump in and start using other people's things. This isn't limited to Twitch and the intellectual property that Twitch provides; it applies to many other things you'll probably use on your broadcast.

The Terms of Service specifically detail what is protected by Twitch: "Twitch's trademarks and logos, the visual interfaces, graphics, design, compilation, information, software, computer code (including source code or object code), services, text, pictures, information, data, sound files, other files." These items are protected under the relevant proprietary rights and laws, meaning that, even though you are using their platform, you may be able to use only the listed items on said platform. Because Twitch can be used worldwide, these words can be interpreted many ways. Since we're talking about a legal document and we are not lawyers, it's always best to consult a lawyer if you fear you may be violating Twitch's copyright or trademark. The only advice we can give you when you think about licensing is that the only thing you own is what you create. This is relevant every time you start a broadcast because, unless your broadcast consists of you sitting in a studio containing only things you created on your own, you are using someone else's product, and there's always a chance that an owner of one of those products may not approve of you using it in your production.

In addition to using products and materials on your broadcast, it's important to note what you are explicitly prohibited from doing with other entities' products and property. The Terms of Service state exactly what you are not allowed to do, such as resell anything with Twitch materials on it, or use mined data that comes straight from the platform itself, via robots or something similar, per our discussion of third-party tools and the like. Remember, by using the Twitch platform you agree to this Terms of Service contract, and breaking it could bring consequences.

Another section is User Content. Because user content has a connection to privacy, a few things come up twice between the User Content and Privacy sections. A bit of legal jargon appears in this section of the agreement, but it generally means that Twitch is allowed to use any content and/or information you put onto the platform for promotional purposes. In the past, Twitch has used short 5- to 10-second clips taken from a creator's video to show off a new feature or event that may launch on Twitch. Often, campaigns like this are planned in cooperation with the creator, but this part of the Terms of Service states that, technically, Twitch doesn't have to do that.

Endorsements and Testimonials

As a broadcaster, you are creating a public product that has the potential to be seen by millions of people all over the world. This means the things you show and talk about on your stream can be perceived as endorsements, and you may be approached to give a testimonial about a product or game. It's also possible you won't be approached for a testimonial at all, and someone may just use what you say on stream however they wish. Obviously, Twitch doesn't permit this unless it's actually Twitch that's using the content. Nevertheless, if something is used even without your permission and is seen by the audience of whoever uses it, that can still reflect on you. The end of the User Content section is mostly about security; this is an important part of your content, which is being broadcast to the public.

When it comes to endorsements, you are obligated to abide by the rules of the Federal Trade Commission, or FTC. As you become a professional in the broadcasting industry, you should familiarize yourself with the guidelines for using testimonials and endorsements in advertising, as well as disclosing such things. We cover this subject in greater detail in Act II of this book. For now, familiarizing yourself with the information the FTC provides is a great way to get started.

Trademarks and Copyrights

Trademarks and copyrights are some of the most widely violated aspects of the broadcasting industry. You may have heard the old adage, touted by Mark Twain, that there's no such thing as a new idea but old ideas that have been rehashed into something that seems new. This may be a culturally embedded ideal that many creators have picked up, especially when they think about their content. Unfortunately for this mindset, the law does not agree, which is why the Terms of Service explicitly state users are prohibited use of Twitch's trademarks and copyrights for outside profit.

In addition to Twitch's trademarks and copyrights, as well as their assets, copyrights exist everywhere, and if you're attempting to run your business and protect your own copyrights, you should do so. Section 10 of Twitch's Terms of Service talks about respecting and protecting copyright. You are empowered by the Digital Millennium Copyright Act, or DMCA, to take action against anyone that may violate your copyright or trademark. Familiarize yourself with the DMCA guidelines to help protect yourself from having your copyright violated or violating someone else's.

Twitch: Creating, Growing, & Monetizing Your Livestream

Written by Dan "danotage" Herrera & Kimberly "Sabre_AP" Weigend

DK/Prima Games, a division of Penguin Random House LLC
6081 East 82nd Street, Suite #400
Indianapolis, IN 46250

ISBN: 978-0-7440-1968-1

Printing Code: The rightmost double-digit number is the year of the book's printing; the rightmost single-digit number is the number of the book's printing. For example, 19-1 shows that the first printing of the book occurred in 2019.

22 21 20 19   4 3 2 1

001-313460-Mar/2019

Printed in Malaysia.

Credits

Publishing Manager
Tim Cox

Book Designer
Darren Strecker

Production
Elisabet Stenberg

Project Manager and Copy Editor
Tim Fitzpatrick

Prima Games Staff

VP & Publisher
Mike Degler

Licensing
Paul Giacomotto

Marketing Manager
Jeff Barton